LIFE *in the* MARBLE PALACE

(IN PRAISE OF FOLLY)

by the Honorable Clifford B. Stearns

[*In Praise of Folly*, written by Erasmus in the early sixteenth century, was one of the most notable works of the Renaissance and one of the catalysts of the Protestant Reformation.]

"Of all men, that distinguish themselves by memorable achievements, the first place of honour seems due to Legislators and founders of states, who transmit a system of laws and institutions to secure the peace, happiness, and liberty of future generations."

David Hume, *Essays, Moral, Political, and Literary* (I, 127.)

 FriesenPress

Suite 300 - 990 Fort St
Victoria, BC, V8V 3K2
Canada

www.friesenpress.com

Copyright © 2016 by Clifford B. Stearns
First Edition — 2016

This book was written over many years while I served in Congress and I would from time to time read an article that I would use as a summary point in my writings. I have not tried to document every source for the ideas in this book. Perhaps my own ideas may parallel these articles in some way, but I tried not to use their language or narrative as my own without identifying where they came from. Albeit I am unable to guarantee this performance because of the length of time I spent in writing this book, I do feel that for the most part I have cited references where my material was obtained.

All rights reserved. No part of this publication may be reproduced in any form, or by any means, electronic or mechanical, including photocopying, recording, or any information browsing, storage, or retrieval system, without permission in writing from FriesenPress.

ISBN
978-1-4602-8760-6 (Hardcover)
978-1-4602-8761-3 (Paperback)
978-1-4602-8762-0 (eBook)

1. BIOGRAPHY & AUTOBIOGRAPHY, PERSONAL MEMOIRS

Distributed to the trade by The Ingram Book Company

Table of Contents

Preface vii
Introduction ix
Timeline xiii

I: Lessons Learned from Getting Elected and Re-elected
Chapter 1: Life in the Marble Palace 1
Chapter 2: Raising Money 5
Chapter 3: Where is God? 9
Chapter 4: Is Majority Rule Always Right? 14
Chapter 5: Debt and Exhaustion 17
Chapter 6: On Freedom 21
Chapter 7: Biggest Bailout in American History 23
Chapter 8: Ousted and a Fact of Life 31
Chapter 9: Publicity and Sound Bites 37
Chapter 10: Freedom and Restraint 41

II: Lessons Learned from Legislating
Chapter 11: Scandals, Ethics, and the War-Lost Majority 45
Chapter 12: The Budget and Awful Numbers No One Believes 51
Chapter 13: The Speaker Dennis Hastert 55
Chapter 14: American Exceptionalism 60
Chapter 15: Opportunity 65
Chapter 16: Who Are You? 67

III: Lessons Learned About Democracy
Chapter 17: Recognizing Good Politics and A Bad Bill, Obamacare . 73
Chapter 18: Impeachment Almost Aborted —
    Newt Gingrich Behind the Scenes 78
Chapter 19: Maintain Republican Control and Majority 82
Chapter 20: The Real Shadow Government 86
Chapter 21: Socialism Around the World 92

Chapter 22: Breeding Contempt for the Law 95
Chapter 23: Does Divine Law Exist? 100
Chapter 24: Limited Government 102
Chapter 25: Travel and Congressional Delegation Trips 108

Conclusion 112
In Praise of Folly: The Solyndra Investigation 119
Appendix 123
Photographs 147
Index 157
About the Author 169
Endnotes 171

Preface

This book was written over many years while I served in Congress; I would, from time to time, read a book or article that I would use as a starting point in my writings. While I was not as careful as I might have been, at the time, when it came to proper citation, great effort has been made during the editing process (years later) to rectify that. I was greatly helped by how far the Internet in general (and Google Books in particular) has come in the meantime.

And lastly, since this book was written over an eight-year cycle and I am only now publishing it, the reader will find that many chapters are written in the present tense, reflecting the time period in which the activities occurred. The message is more effective written as it occurs as opposed to from a historical perspective. I hope this is not a distraction but will give a feel and understanding of what was felt and occurred at that moment.

As always, my greatest thanks go to my wife, Joan, who provided encouragement to me to continue writing and, ultimately, to get this book published. And I might add, she encouraged me to run for Congress in the first place. I almost didn't without her push!

Introduction

Historically, the House of Representatives has been divided into three parties, namely Republican, Democrat, and Independents—though as of the writing of this introduction, there hasn't been an Independent in the House since 2007. Regardless of party affiliation, all members of the House have to compromise at times and end up feeling like they have strayed.

In the Senate, they are often free of this strict party affiliation. The Senate is considered the "most exclusive assisted living club in America." For sure there is the prestige of this club, and any one Senator can stop a bill. But the *real* power is in the House. It is the best job in America. This is a story about serving in the House, why it is such a wonderful job, and what needs to be done to make it work! It's more fun than the Senate, and a whole lot safer if you can just keep your head.

All money is appropriated in the House, and the decision to make war is also initiated in the House. Impeachment of the president (POTUS) also begins there. The House was also entrusted, by the Framers, with the power to rein in the abuses of the Executive and Judicial branches through investigations and impeachments. Congress can also limit the appellate jurisdiction of the Supreme Court and, if necessary, dismantle any court inferior to the Supreme Court. The House was intended to be the most accountable of the federal government (since its members stand for election every two years) with the power of the purse, which is now over $4 trillion a year!

By controlling the power of the purse, the House has the means to shut down all federal activities that undermine our constitutional order. Combine that with our enormous GDP and military power in the world, and you get an idea of the extent of this power. Our cultural influence is vast, and most countries cannot stop it from pervading theirs. As a member of the House, you are on the board of the most powerful body in the world—the United States of America. In a nutshell, we are the Prince of Power in all of history.

It is such an honor to be a member of Congress. It is a sacred responsibility. Aristotle, when asked about the best form of life one could live, suggested that *eudaimonia* [happiness]† could best be pursued as a lawgiver.¹ Not the billionaire, not the priest or saint or health giver, but the legislator.

Why? Because he is immersed in the political needs and realities of his time and contributing to the *polis* [Greek city-state] through legislative activity and through his own virtuous conduct. He then can contribute in such a way that the polis—like a person—perfects itself by regulating itself more perfectly through the principles and tenets of reason, proportionality, prudence, balance, harmony, fitness, and aptness. He calls the rule of reason a royal rule, a princely rule.

So you have the power of money—because Lord knows you spend and appropriate it in the billions—and you have the power to help countless persons, institutions, and ultimately, your country. You are not altogether famous, but rather a minor celebrity. So you have fame, unless you get caught in a scandal, and then you are lost. This brings one to the third desirous felicitation: love. This should come from the love of the job as well the adulation of the public. Unfortunately the latter often feeds on itself, fueling scandal and the loss of everything.

And lastly, you are part of the great debate dealing with the value of Western civilization. One of the most fundamental features of Western thought is faith in human progress and in man's capacity to create a world of justice and peace. This hope has its roots both in Greek and in Roman thinking, as well as in messianic Old Testament prophets. History is unfolding.

The prophetic concept was a historical one, a state of perfection to be realized by man within historical time. Christianity transformed this concept into a spiritual one. Our founding fathers did not create a classical republic but a new kind of republic, as outlined in the *Federalist Papers*. This new republic did not try to stifle the factions or moneyed interest groups from competing, but disperse their power so that they could not dominate the minority or become the constant majority.

The march of freedom is that ultimate perfection which Aristotle talked about. With America, we have the first nation in human history that is not intent on conquering but on liberating and allowing all nations the freedom and markets to reach their own height of perfection. But with that freedom comes choices. As Edmund Burke put it, "What is liberty without wisdom and without virtue? It is the greatest of all possible evils." Or as Tocqueville put it, "Freedom is, in truth, a sacred thing. There is only one thing else that better deserves the name: That is virtue. But what is virtue if not the free choice of what is good?"

And that choice is what we, in Congress, want all nations to have. But we are now engaged in a battle with others who believe that liberty is derived from the Koran and that you cannot separate church and state and allow religious freedom. To these persons of extreme religious fervor, they believe that democracy is a sin because it is man's laws and not God's.

But alas, an overriding issue for our nation and its historical destiny is that no democracy and/or republic has lasted *more than 240* years. For us to survive, our country has to be restored. From my vantage point of twenty-four years of service in this House, I see many problems and flaws that may indeed lead to our collapse.

This reconquest can begin in the House and may be the only way to really win the war to continue and sustain our republic. This story may help to do that. To view the day-to-day activities of a congressman and his attempt to rise above what Cicero described as "perverse bidding wars in which candidates seek to curry favor with the masses by bribing them with other people's property" may indeed provide insight to restore our republic. The governmental "benevolence" which is paid for by confiscated wealth and stolen liberties is always part of politics. But ultimately it must stop, or elections will continue to become electoral plunder and not the virtuous balance of reason that leads to Aristotle's princely rule.

So our story begins.

———

* From *Oxford Dictionary of Philosophy* by Simon Blackburn.

Eudaimonia: (Greek, happiness, well-being, success) The central goal of all systems of ancient ethics; according to Aristotle, the 'best, noblest, and most pleasant thing in the world.' Eudaimonia is a placeholder waiting for further specification, and different ethical theories will fill it out differently. Aristotle conceives of it as the active exercise of the powers of the (virtuous) soul in conformity to reason. Eudaimonia is usually translated as happiness or well-being, but it has some of the same connotations as 'success,' since in addition to living well it includes doing well. For example, it can be diminished by events that happen after the subject's death, and it is not a state that children can possess. It is complete and self-sufficient, to be attained for no other end than itself, so it includes all other ends that are pursued for themselves. It therefore includes pleasure, but goes beyond it. In Book X of the *Nicomachean Ethics*, Aristotle extols the life of study as the essential realization of eudaimonia.

Timeline

Major events occurring during Congressman Cliff Stearns' career:

[**April–June 1989**] Tiananmen Square protests, Beijing

[**Nov. 1989**] *Fall* of the Berlin Wall

[**Sept. 1990**] President George H.W. Bush increased taxes in 1990 budget agreement

[**Oct. 1990**] Reunification of Germany

[**Aug. 1990–Feb. 1991**] *The* Gulf War (Desert Shield & Desert Storm)

[**Dec. 1991**] Collapse of the Soviet Union

[**Nov. 1992**] Bill Clinton elected president

[**Jan. 1994**] North American Free Trade Act (NAFTA) signed into law by President Clinton

[**Apr. 1994**] South Africa ends apartheid

[**Jan. 1995**] Republicans take control of the House of Representatives, first time in 40 years

[**Nov. 1996**] President Bill Clinton re-elected

[**Dec. 1998**] Impeachment of President Clinton

[**Nov. 2000**] George W. Bush elected president

[**Sept. 2001**] 9/11 terrorist attacks in New York City, Shanksville, Pa., and, Va.

[**Oct. 2001**] War in Afghanistan started

[**Mar. 2003**] Second war in Iraq launched by President George W. Bush

[**Nov. 2004**] President George W. Bush re-elected 2004

[**Jan. 2007**] Democrats retake control of the House of Representatives

[**Dec. 2007**] The United States entered its longest post-World War II recession

[**Nov. 2008**] President Obama elected

[**Mar. 2010**] Patient Protection and Affordable Care Act or "Obamacare" signed into law

[**2010-2011**] Arab Spring originated in Tunisia in December 2010 and quickly took hold in Egypt, Libya, Syria, Yemen, Bahrain, Saudi Arabia, and Jordan in 2011

[**Jan. 2011**] Republicans regained control of the House; Democrats lose a total of 63 seats

[**May 2011**] Osama bin Laden killed in Pakistan

[**Oct. 2011**] President Obama ordered the end of U.S. military involvement in Iraq

[**Nov 2012**] President Obama re-elected

I
Lessons Learned from Getting Elected and Re-elected

Chapter 1
Life in the Marble Palace

DECIDE EARLY WHAT YOU WANT

From the first moment you get elected to any office, in particular as a member of Congress, you must decide what you want to do with that office. You have several immediate options. It is a slippery slope if you delay your decisions. If you want to make a career of being a member of Congress, you must decide early, and that can be a good thing. There is an election every two years, but with it comes the opportunity to enjoy the use of power and the ability to help people. And the longer you stay in Congress, the more power you obtain—even as a minority member of Congress. Your seniority allows you the chance to become a subcommittee chairman with legal counsel and special staff or a full committee chairman with a host of issues that impact not just the United States but also the world. Also, you have a world of issues to choose from, whether it is foreign affairs or telecommunications, transportation, energy, judiciary, taxes or simply spending $4.5 trillion as a member of the budget committee or appropriation committees.

All during this process, you will have to raise money for other members and work the intra-party politics of your colleagues to be able to advance. So even within this decision process to stay as an incumbent congressman, you will have challenges to reach your goal. But if your decision is to run for higher office, then it is not to your advantage to stay more than four terms or eight years—twelve years at the most. But the decision to leave Congress is very important because, in most cases, you cannot return. The opportunities will be forever closed off to you. I have seen so many members seek higher office and lose and want to come back.

Dan Lungren, the former attorney general for the state of California, made it back after losing in a run for the Senate and governor. He is the exception. Many members who try, after realizing what a magnificent job it is, want to come back and lose in a primary. Almost all people who leave miss the office and the special privileges that go with being a member of Congress (MC). One former member of California spent $6.5 million of his own money only to lose to a state Senator, Tom McClintock, in the primary for a Republican House Seat. He was on Ways and Means, the premier committee in Congress, when he left because he said he was tired of the job! Nowhere else do you have the audience and the opportunity to affect the world as a MC *or Senator*. So the decision to leave must be weighed very carefully.

If you want to leave to make more money, then that is one thing. It is easy to do as a lobbyist or as a CEO of an association of companies that need lobby work in Congress. You can make from $350,000 up to $2 million depending upon your education, political skills, and competence. After a career in Congress, you have developed a lot of skills and contacts that will help many businesses. Plus, you still have contacts in Congress that will allow you access on very important issues.

If, however, you want to run for higher office, then that decision requires a different approach. Every member is careful how he votes and tries his best to represent his constituents, his own moral values, and what he feels is best for America. However, there are certain votes dealing with fiscal responsibility and defense that can make a difference in a statewide race. Every member who is in Congress is interested in higher office. And he will have many opportunities to do so. What he must decide is when to do so. If he can avoid a primary, that is desirable. But he must husband his campaign funds, forget about helping other members and his party, and keep his money raised for his run for higher office. Transferring over a million dollars to your Senate or governor's race puts you way ahead of the curve, and it is intimidating to opponents. Instead of complying with your leadership with money and time, you have to be selfish and keep your mission in mind. Vote with running for high office in your state in mind, and garner your campaign funds.

Start early to get around the state, and remember that you might have to run more than once to eventually win a statewide race. It makes no sense to spend a lot of time in DC. Go home every weekend, and make contacts. While staying in DC and working the politics there will help you advance in your committee assignments in Congress, it will not help you win a statewide race. The best example is Mark Sanford (became Governor of South Carolina and, after his scandal, returned to Congress) who voted against almost everything and slept in his office his whole time of eight years on Congress. He made no effort to work with his colleagues or even get to know them. He left after his pledge of term limits. If I had wanted to run for higher office, I should have left after twelve years when I talked about term limits while running in my first term. But I enjoyed the job, and knew that I would not have this amount of intellectual stimulation and enjoyment even as a governor or senator. Both other jobs are more demanding but offer different challenges. The Senate is lonely and a club of independents who generally want to run for president. Being a governor is very desirable, but it is about working on crafting a budget and not changing things beyond your state. There are no national issues and little time for the wide range of traveling that a congressman is offered.

So in conclusion, one has to decide early what he wants to do. Make money after a career in Congress, go up the ladder of responsibility in the House of Representatives, or seek higher office. In all cases, the decision must be made early and requires a different modus operandi as one adapts to being a member of Congress. But one should realize that a lot of good men and women have thrown off the mantle of congressperson to run for higher office only to regret it for the rest of their lives—many have sought to come back but to no avail. When you have achieved something special, you have to carefully weigh the benefit and rewards. A career as a member of Congress is certainly more than satisfactory.

Chapter 2
Raising Money

THE BANE OF YOUR EXISTENCE

Fundraising enters into every part of life. Whether you are a community college president or four-year university president, you have to raise money. If you are prominent in your community, you most likely will take on the chairmanship of United Way and have to raise money. The local foundation for your community hospital or the local Boys & Girls Club is going to need your service.

However, nothing compares to raising money for your own personal campaign, a campaign in which you can never raise *enough* money. In a typical congressional campaign in an open seat, you may have to raise $4 million. One member from Florida spent $5.5 million of his own money, and only 300 votes elected him. Typically as an incumbent, you will spend between $450,000 and $650,000 against a weak opponent. Invariably, there is a feeling that the incumbent has to prove himself, and most voters' loyalty is paper-thin—they always think someone new will do a better job. I am not sure why, but it is hard to satisfy all the people all the time, and like being a television or movie star, your popularity wanes as time goes on. So it is a constant effort. In some congressional districts, it is easy to win, and you do not have to spend a lot of money because the voter registration is solid Republican or Democrat.

For those times when you have to face off against a strong opponent, you will have to raise at least $3 million. And remember, your contributors are limited in the amount they can give, and they cannot write off these contributions on their taxes. So you will have to line up folks who feel strongly about the political issues and really like what you are doing.

There is nothing more gut-wrenching than to see your opponent raise more money than you. Some members do suppers and breakfast meetings for fundraising, and others spend a lot of money on direct mail. But the easiest way to raise it is to have a large event and bring down a celebrity like the President of the United States (POTUS) or leadership members from your party. This is a lot of fun, but a lot of work. Assuming you can get 500 people to attend at $200 per person, you can raise $100,000. If this same event is put into a two-tiered event, you can raise almost double. Simply allow a photo with the VIP or celebrity for a higher amount.

There was one congressman who never spent more than $10,000 in a cycle. Bill Natcher (D-Kentucky) refused to accept campaign contributions. He was Chairman of the House Appropriations Committee from 1993 to 1994. He also never missed a vote. In fact, he was brought in on a stretcher from the Bethesda Naval Hospital for a last series of votes in the evening. He was a courtly gentleman, but also a good illustration of what is otherwise accepted wisdom: you will want to miss some votes, so you do not feel pressured to make every vote. So miss that one vote early!

At any rate, Congressman Natcher once told me that his campaign strategy was simple. He only placed ads in the newspapers. He did not bother with TV or radio, but went around to all the newspapers and visited with the editorial boards. What he felt was most important was to visit with all the local merchants downtown in all his counties. He walked in unannounced and asked for the owner and talked to them about what he was doing in Congress and how he was helping the county and his town. He just made contact and kept his reputation as a regular guy who had not left his roots. He was always polite and kind. He really was never partisan on the floor. He held office in a time when you did not have to give money to the national parties to get your chairmanship. Also, there was not pressure to give to other members in the typical "breakout" fund they always put you through. You did not have to give money from your campaign fund for the president's or *leader's* big supper at the DC Convention Center for the political party's biannual fundraising event. This last event is always a chore. Most of the money will come in from the PACs anyway if they want to have influence, and you generally have to put pressure on your state folks through individual contributions.

Before Congressman Gingrich was in leadership, the fundraising effort was minimal. But after he became Speaker, he moved it to a new level.

As chairman of a major committee, you had to raise $1.5 million or more to be competitive. So you had to have a leadership fund to develop individual giving to members, especially open seats so they would support you. When the steering committee met after the election, you had to show how much money you raised for the party and how much money you gave out to individual members. There are exceptions to the rule on who finally got a chairmanship. Admittedly, Representative Peter King of New York raised little money to get chairmanship of the new Homeland Security Committee, but generally it was given to the member who raised the most money.

Leadership is decided by who can raise and give the most money—not the most competitive or competent or best speaker or most politically astute, but who is able to raise the mega bucks. And when you think about it, those members from large cities have an advantage initially.

Raising money is done by making tons of phone calls—or soliciting a fundraiser to do it for you. Fundraisers line up the calls and make the event dates and schedule everything. But they generally take twenty to twenty-five percent of the gross. They will also set up the event so that all you have to do is show up.

But as mentioned earlier, scandals arise because of this constant raising of money. When you think about it, whoever gives you money is going to expect something for it. They will not ask for it immediately, but sometime in the near future, you can count on it. It is not merely access they want, but also *influence* at the table. So both parties have to take that into consideration when they accept that money. That is why almost every member would like to see a real campaign finance bill that puts a ceiling on campaign contributions, much like they do in Canada and the UK. In Canada, the elect run a campaign for under $50,000 and spend it all. In Britain it is about the same. This is so that the incumbent does not have the huge advantage over challengers.

An incumbent is known and recognized, so why does he need so much money to run? Grant a couple of TV debates to the challenger—let's make that mandatory and call it a day. Let all the newspapers and radio stations interview the candidates, and in less *than* two months, the public will know all they need to know about a challenger. Charges and counter-charges and negative campaigning can still exist, but it is through the media and perhaps a few direct mail pieces that candidates should make their case. *Someday* a real campaign finance bill will emerge, and when that happens, corruption and undue influence of legislation will cease.

The sooner the better.

Chapter 3
Where is God?

I am reminded, whenever I vote, that there must be a right and wrong to every vote. True, there is compromise in the House of Representatives, but even with compromise, there must be a right and wrong. Maybe sometimes one should just vote "present," but I doubt it.

Two things strike me when I think about this. Is there a divine retribution if votes are cast that go against universal rules, whether that be Kant's categorical imperative or scriptural interpretation? And how long before that retribution moves in on an individual and a nation?

Kant's categorical imperative is straightforward:

"Make no law that *cannot* be universally applied to everyone in the world."

When you hold to that, it would seem easy to vote. But then you must consider three other things: your district or your constituents, your own personal feelings, and lastly, what is good for the nation. Generally the main consideration that prevails is getting reelected, especially if you have an election in five months. Oftentimes I wonder if the citizens of this country care enough to properly follow what we do to ensure that a member votes appropriately.

Is there divine punishment for an individual or nation that does not obey God's laws, universal laws, Kant's laws and/or natural law?

I view it first from the Scriptures. In both the New and Old Testament, there is punishment and severe repercussions if religious admonitions are not heeded.[2] Here are a few examples from the Old

Testament: The theme of God's punishment can be found from beginning to end in the Bible. Even if you do not believe in God, from the history of the Bible we see in the Book of Genesis chastisement for sin: Tower of Babel, the flood, the enslavement of the children of Israel, their long wandering in the desert and subsequent division of King David's kingdom after Saul into two different kingdoms that continually feud.

In the New Testament there are also examples. In the Acts of the Apostles, two people—Ananias and Sapphira—are struck dead when they disobey the code and keep private property for themselves. From a biblical standpoint, divine punishment exists.

The twelfth chapter of the Letter to the Hebrews is clear in regard to this question: "My sons, do not disdain the discipline of the Lord nor lose heart when He reproves you; for whom the Lord loves, he disciplines; he scourges every son he receives" (Heb. 12:6).

With divine punishment comes education and then love. God's discipline is always a disciplining born of love, a type of formation for the recalcitrant soul. Just like a father disciplines his son, so does God. If in fact a father truly loves his son, he will discipline him. We call it tough love. Because we sin, God disciplines in a harsh and dreadful way. So what must be true for a family is true on a large scale. For a nation that disobeys the natural law, the law of universal application and the spiritual law, there will be consequences.

If a nation contravenes the divinely established order at the ethical level, it will face divine punishment as a result. God's tough love. That is what the Congress and the White House are experiencing now. And the question is, will our nation suffer, too? The good news is that, after this punishment, there is brought forth the fruit of peace and justice for those who learn the lessons.

Life is all about learning lessons. If one does not learn them, then life gets harder and harder until one is forced to learn them.

But is all suffering the result of divine judgment? Not all. In the Book of Job, we can see that a righteous man without sin also is punished.

But like every other endeavor in life, politics can see divine punishment occur and with it, suffering. Expressions of tough love from

God are indeed indication that we are undergoing training in the divine school.

But in the end, from a spiritual standpoint, one has to also see a lot of bad things happen to good people who might just get caught up in the swing of scandal.

You can also look at it from another standpoint. If you can discern the natural law for any given situation, then you will realize that these laws require obedience. And people and nations will suffer unwanted results even for an inadvertent attempt to disobey what natural law decrees. So, only right actions get right results. If a nation or a person finds wrong results and chaos wreaks havoc in the nation and people's lives, then they know their thinking and behavior are wrong.

In his famous book *As A Man Thinketh*, James Allen aptly points out that all that a person achieves is the result of his thoughts.[3] So must it be with a nation. If a nation's thoughts or attitude or cosmic awareness is wrong, then its behavior must in turn be wrong.

As a legislator, how do I ensure my thoughts and behavior are correct and that the legislation that I sponsor and vote for is *correct*? If a man and a nation are literally what they think, then what is my role? Bad legislation corrupts a nation, and good legislation makes a nation survive.

Do I withdraw support from what I perceive as wrong actions and vote against such legislation? Yes. But how am I to be sure?

Oftentimes, when I do my town meetings, I find many of the citizens are emotional and reason from distortions of logic; they are only thinking of themselves and are out of touch with the common reality of the universal good. That is where I come in and think as a representative and must vote not just in pursuit of parochial interests.

In some sense, all wrong actions could also be considered premeditated because, initially, it takes wrong thought to cause wrong action in the first place. So in the end, I believe right action cannot produce wrong results. But this right thinking cannot be always discerned, and there is a higher power driving and supporting the ultimate success. But honestly, no one knows then what will happen. We know today that right action and ethical behavior comes from a person's thinking, and that is a vital factor in the emotional and physical status of a person's health.[4]

I am reminded when I vote, then, of both the spiritual and the temporal laws. "Take right action regarding every natural law, and if you do not, you will incur wrong, unwanted results."[5] So it must be with legislation that is passed in Congress. I believe, in many respects, there must be a law of absolute right and that, as legislators, we must be held accountable for whatever happens to this nation.

Which brings me to the crux of the matter—how to vote so that I am not corrupted and neither is the nation. And if it turns out that my *no* vote does not defeat a proposal, then at least I am not part of an evil or faulty designed system of legislation.

So they say there is a separation of church and state, but how can it be if you are to do what is right? Before Christianity, the Jews discerned what was right. Before the Jews, the Greeks were able *to build* a nation on doing what is right and *likewise* so did Rome. And so many other civilizations were able to keep a strong, safe nation and influence the world … not necessarily based upon God but these natural laws of nature and personal behavior.

Even as far back 40 A.D., Seneca, in his work *On the Shortness of Life*, talked about this natural law when he said, "We labor in vain against nature's opposition."[6] He went on to say, "He who fears death will never do anything worthy of a living man."[7]

Likewise, he who is afraid to lose an election will never be able to do what is right.

History of Nations

Before leaving the subject of divine punishment, it may be useful to look at history from Herodotus. A major theme of the Histories of Herodotus is the way in which time can effect surprising changes in the fortunes and reputations of empires, cities and men. Should we forget divine punishment and just consider the prevalent ethos that all nations rise and then fall, then it is just matter of time before a nation falls.[8]

Herodotus is neutral on the relative merits of monarchy, oligarchy, and democracy; in a passage known as "Debate on Government," he has critical things to say about all three. So maybe there is no answer—governments just fall in time, and no government is perfect. Early in his Histories, he makes reference to the way in which cities and states rise and fall. Suddenly, there may be a natural principle involved. Says Herodotus, "And so, resting on my knowledge that human prosperity never remains constant ..." he makes warning of imperial ambition. The fate of the Persians is an object lesson for all nations.

For Herodotus, virtually everything can be assimilated into a kind of natural cycle of checks and balances. He attempts to give a picture of the world entirely, or how everything in it is essentially linked. So if all is linked from his standpoint, then every action has impact for good or evil.

The concept in Latin is that of *ta genomena ex anthropon* [things that result from human actions].

So as old is his writings are, they are remarkably familiar and even contemporary in their relevance to us today. His readings are many generations from us, but there is much to learn from him, for he describes the way things work out and how it is generally the fault of the participants.

Chapter 4
Is Majority Rule Always Right?

It is often said that two major factors contributed to the development of the United States and its culture. The first is the rationalism of the eighteenth century, and the other is the Protestant Reformation. We see this independent spirit expressed in the eighteenth century Gadsden flag with its motto: *Don't tread on me*. That feeling is still prevalent today and goes to the heart of who we are.

That is our freedom of choice and self-determination. To be free is to be able to say yes or no to everything we do. But what does this freedom mean if we are not able to make the right choice? We have this choice, and how does this apply to a democracy? Do we give everybody this choice even when it is the majority's rule and the majority is wrong? Everybody wants to decide for oneself. And the majority in Congress wants to do the same thing. Make that choice.

But as pointed out by others, there is an older understanding of this word freedom. Freedom from ancient philosophy and the Bible.

This could be termed "freedom for excellence," and this freedom can be interpreted to mean that freedom "is not so much individual choice as the disciplining of desire so as to make the achievement of the good, first possible, and then effortless."[9] You can say whatever you want on the House floor, but what you say and how you say it successfully will depend upon discipline and exercise of your skills, for example.

So the first type of freedom is historically a law and a claim to the objective truth that you have this right of choice and self-actualization in your life. Better said by the Declaration of Independence:

> We hold these truths to be self-evident, that all men are created equal, that they are endowed by their Creator with certain unalienable *Rights, that* among these are Life, Liberty, and the pursuit of Happiness.

"When Thomas Jefferson referred in the Declaration of Independence to "unalienable rights" endowed by the Creator, he radically popularized—if not created himself—a category that barely exists in scripture or history. Certainly 'life, liberty, and the pursuit of happiness' are not unalienable—that is, 'not to be separated, given away, or taken away.' In the eighteenth century these three, along with certain though unnamed others, were routinely taken away by due process in Jefferson's colonial America."[10]

But the second type of freedom positively requires the law and the good, for it finds itself in surrendering to them. The difference between these two freedoms comes into play when the majority rules. You can see this in Supreme Court decisions.

From a religious point of view, it is summed up by Paul in his Epistle to the Galatians. "It is for freedom that Christ has set you free" (Gal 5:1). He goes on in his Letter to the Romans to present himself as "Paul, a slave of Christ Jesus" (Rom 1:1). So there is correlation between freedom and truth from a biblical standpoint.

Would Plato, Aristotle, or Cicero have thought, as Jefferson did, that it is self-evident that all people are fundamentally equal and endowed with inviolable rights? I doubt that they would. In Plato's *Republic*, he argues for the best people to rule. He wanted excellence. Likewise with Aristotle's *Politics*—he wanted only a handful of bright people to participate in public life.

Without the clear reference to the Creator God in Jefferson's declaration, political convictions become somewhat less than self-evident. Totalitarian rule by the majority occurred initially with Nazism and Communism.

So what it all comes down to is, what is truth? Does modern democracy always provide the truth with majority rule?

I fear the answer is no.

Does the ever-evolving consensus of the people provide for truth?[11]

And so the dilemma is thus: is it really possible to be a believer in the revealed truth and accept majority rule? Pontius Pilate was the prototype of the modern democrat. He allowed the majority to rule, and despite his personal feelings, he was willing to go along with the stated consensus of the majority. He was the avatar who made a decision based upon the correct democratic procedures and not on objective good.

The truth you find after voting, time and time again, is not the majority opinion of good government and cannot be conditioned by the decision of government. Oftentimes a member becomes a corrupt coward by voting with the majority instead of going against the herd mentality.

"Freedom is indeed a great and abiding value within a democratic polity, but real freedom must be maintained in constant correlation to the truth, lest it devolve into libertinism. The free decisions of a democratic society—mediated politically by the elected government—must take place within the context of a network of truths and moral values that are not themselves subject to vote."[12]

To get elected officials to exercise the right vote requires that they have a mystical intuition or right values. Where the member gets these values is important, and the Church must articulate, in a public way, the moral context for any and all government activity and raise its voice when practical politics works against the rights of individuals.

Back during the founding of this country, churches in America spoke out on issues of the day. A good example was John Witherspoon, President of Princeton, who spoke freely on civil rights during the eighteenth century.

Chapter 5
Debt and Exhaustion

When you finally get through all the primaries and inch by with a general election win, you are exhausted and in debt. For members who do not have prior political experience, it is like walking to the edge of a cliff. Either you have mortgaged your house or you have spent all the cash you had, and no sooner do you get elected than you are faced with the full-time effort of paying yourself back. It is truly a management nightmare. Sure, everyone congratulates you, but your spouse is totally disarranged, and *your marriage is stressed.*

Your children enjoy the new celebrity status, but they soon undergo stress once you are gone and all semblance of routine is broken. Most members end their campaigns in debt anywhere from $250,000 to as much as $5 million. Even if you are wealthy, it is still a challenging experience.

The first thing you have to do is to jockey for position in your class and seek the right committee assignments that will help you in your district (but also pay back your debt). Your classmates, whether they be Democrat or Republican, are your so-call friends, but you will find out soon enough that oftentimes they want the same committees and positions you do. Who will be the president of your class, whip, and most importantly, get elected to the steering committee, which decides who goes where? In every class, there is one person who gets elected by the class to the extremely important steering committee.

The steering committee is the ultimate power position for a freshman. I got elected from a hospital bed in the Bethesda Naval Hospital, suffering from prostatitis and a high fever after three elections over five months. With this position, every member in your party (even senior members) suddenly knows your name and wants your vote for what he or she wants in new committee assignments. They also think you can persuade your freshman class to support them for leadership positions, which also are determined at the start of each session. So you spend a lot time trying to decide who to vote for and trying to get your own positions without revealing your ambition. Ambitious people are rarely successful because, among politicians, personal relationships are what works and not self-centered ambitious people. Except that, if you can raise the money, then personal relationships get trumped when someone maxes out in your campaign. That person you do not forget.

The steering committee is made of the following, and it is pretty much the same operation for both parties. Independents generally go with one of the two parties. The structure and votes available are as such:

The Speaker or Leader	5
Whip	2
Deputy Whip	1
Chairman	1
Energy & Commerce	1
Ways and Means	1
Appropriations	1
Science and Tech	1
Banking & Financial	1
At Large	1
Freshman class representative	1
Junior class representative	1
Small States	1
Large States	1

You do not want to make any of these members mad. It is a secret ballot, and the members trade for their designees, and you can be lost in the shuffle. Decisions made at that steering committee could affect you for the rest of your career. There are members with twenty years of service who vividly remember when they got screwed by the steering committee and will always remember who was responsible.

The hard part is who to support for the leadership positions, and often the decision is made for you by senior members whose help you need to secure advancement.

Once you get the committee you get (whether it is the one you wanted or not), you are faced with a huge education and orientation on what that committee is all about. You have to decide what your priorities are and what bills you want to sponsor so the folks back home know you are accomplishing something. But all you *really* want to do is sleep.

Raising money is a constant. If you don't show a strong fundraising effort, you will surely be in for a tough general election. I had a primary challenge into my second term. But if you can raise sufficient money early, you can scare off serious candidates. I also found lots of town meetings shows your work effort. I did as many as twelve town meetings in one day. I brought along a camera crew from my campaign to put it into a commercial so I could show I was not a slacker.

The constant fundraisers are a real drag. Standing around and talking endlessly with people you hardly know, hoping they will give money is tiresome. Sometimes you meet someone you generally like. But it is all the same whether you're running for the House or the Senate or even for presidency. Endless fundraising and setting up individual fundraising in the district. Many members enjoy constant calling on the phone. I rarely did, but I did it. Plus you have to do it for your party e.g., President's dinner, party fundraisers, etc. But after a while, you get *used* to it, and sometimes you start to enjoy it.

But there is one outstanding moment for a freshman, particularly one who has not served at the state level—the moment when you are on the House floor voting for the first time. Four hundred thirty-five names are hidden behind a thin tapestry over the speaker's chair, and it stretches across the width of the House. When that vote is called, a switch turns on the names of all 435 members, and there is blank space beside their name. Bingo green and red lights flash across this wall as members start to vote. The ballot versus the bullet. It is awe-inspiring. You can also vote "present" (the color is yellow).

I will never forget my first time voting. I kept saying to myself, *Here I am in the most powerful country in the world, the biggest economy, and the superpower. Is God in this chamber? Where else would he be if not here? Is every vote predicated upon an absolute right or wrong, and will I see it clearly? If God is here, then the devil is not far behind.*

Little did I know of the enormous temptation, immorality, and ethical challenges of this place. Would I be able to resist party *pressure? How* do you make the right decision for your district, your country, and your personal inclinations? Balancing all three would forever be a challenge. And I wanted to be true to my supporters and not let them down. So often, members voted for power, money contributions, or personal advancement.

Oh, this is the USA.

How long will she be? She is not a classical republic but a *new* republic, where competing factions are brought together to keep power disbursed. *Every American should read article 10 of The Federalist Papers.*

Chapter 6
On Freedom

(AFTER READING *THE MONK WHO SOLD HIS FERRARI*[13] BY ROBIN S. SHARMA)

When one talks about the freedom or liberty that our forefathers expressed in the Declaration of Independence or the Constitution, it's clear that they did not tell the entire story on this concept.

And this becomes a problem when you liberate countries such as Iraq or Afghanistan.

With this initial freedom, the liberated people can go where they want and do what they want. But if you are a slave to your impulses, and these impulses are based upon bad habits, you will do bad things with eventual consequences. People think they can go wherever they want after being set free. So in a way, a person without discipline and self-control will have liberty but not true freedom. We as a nation must explain that to newly freed citizens. We probably need to explain to our own people.

You must forge freedom into the freedom to choose what is right over what seems pressing or merely pleasing or, in many cases, prurient. Is one always putting out fires and not seeing the forest for the trees without time to truly communicate with loved ones? Oftentimes, we can't seem to break habits that are killing us, whether harmful to our body or mind. Are we slaves to our impulses? It is the building of willpower that will make one more free because, in the end, you live the life you have imagined for yourself rather than accepting the life that you have been dealt. In this way, one can erase the worry habit and ultimately ease one's mind and give one more energy.

Chapter 7
Biggest Bailout in American History

UNDER REPUBLICAN PRESIDENT'S WATCH!

It is very difficult for me to comprehend how this could happen. Republicans are free-marketers, yet under the twelve years of Republican control of the House, we did not curb the excesses. The Secretary of Treasury Paulson was on the job for almost two years and was the former CEO of Goldman Sachs. He must have known about the abuses of his colleagues at Bear Stearns and Lehman Brothers. He was in a near panic and wanted Congress to give him sole authority to spend almost a trillion dollars without any strings attached. His hubris was without limit, and his scratchy voice all the more surrealistic as he spoke to our conference asking for the TARP bailout of $750 million in 2008.

Two weeks prior, I attempted to transfer all of my campaign funds, IRA and personal accounts for the family to T. R. Price. After two weeks of trying, I was advised by Morgan Stanley that it would not occur until October 16, or almost a month after this was initiated by me as an electronic transfer. Former member of Congress called me to help a friend who lives in Orlando to help him get his money out of a Reserve Primary Fund money market, which is the oldest money market fund in existence. It had 1.2% of its assets invested in Lehman Brothers, and when it went bankrupt, there was a run on the fund. The

Treasury Department guaranteed the assets of all money funds with a net asset value of at least one dollar as of September 17, 2008. The Reserve Primary Fund had an asset value of $.97 on that date, so it didn't qualify for the guarantee. The Fund was frozen by the Treasury *Dept.* to prevent a further run on it.

This was starting to be a problem. We can debate how we got into this problem, but that will not help us now. As George Will said, "Everything that has been done for the last six months has been done to cope with what previous actions were supposed to prevent."[14]

So what was the big rush? I could not help but feel that a simple solution to this problem was to do what we did during the Savings and Loan crisis in 1989 and the early nineties. Speaker Pelosi and I both served on the Banking Committee at that time, and we were both on the Senate/House conference to work out the final bill. We had hearings on this legislation, and we also had markups and free discussions. Yet during that time, we were never told that only one man could spend almost one trillion dollars without Congressional oversight. My phone calls on this matter were running 400 to 1 *against* this bailout. What we did in the S&L crisis is eerily familiar.

The Federal Deposit Insurance Corp. took care of Washington Mutual, now the largest bank failure in history, in an orderly manner, with no cost to the FDIC or taxpayers. So we were able to resolve banking failure without taxpayer's money in a time-tested manner. So if the problem then was that the public, including Wall Street, was getting scared and starting to panic, why didn't we allow the FDIC to go into the failed institutions and handle them like we did Washington Mutual and advise the public it will protect all depositors and other general creditors?

Based upon the scare tactics used by the Secretary of Treasury and the Federal Reserve Chairman when they bought Bear Stearns, took over *Freddie Mac* [Federal Home Loan Mortgage Corporation], *Fannie Mae* [Federal National Mortgage Association] and AIG, what assurance did we have that, after they spend *$750* billion, we will have solved the problem? We needed a temporary program to calm depositors, which could be the role of FDIC. Secretary Paulson's plan assumed the government could sell off these loans without disrupting the market further. Having the government purchase loans at inflated prices and then sell the loans to others at deflated prices is not a good deal for the taxpayers.

Why not make a loan to these institutions and ask for interest on returns for these loans, much like we did for the loans to NYC and Chrysler for those bailouts? We eventually made money. The FDIC resolved a $100 billion insolvency in the savings banks for a total cost of *less than* $2 billion.[15] This plan would have allowed the institutions time to sell and restructure their assets and get on with their own survival. No taxpayer money would be spent, and fair market value for the bad loans would be established rather than the government upsetting the establishment of this fair market value. These sales would remain in the private sector where they belong.

As also suggested by *Mr. William Isaac,* this type of program would (1) ease the fears of the depositors and general creditors of banks; (2) keep tight restrictions on short sellers of financial stocks; (3) suspend fair-value accounting, which has contributed mightily to our problems by marking assets to unrealistic fire-sale prices; and (4) authorize a new worth certificate program, and we could settle the financial markets without significant expense to taxpayers.[15]

We do NOT need taxpayers to carry their bad loans. We just need time to work through these problems and put in place regulatory and accounting policies that will give the needed time.

The decision to allow our government to nationalize our banks and to take over these bad loans in America goes against the very grain of all that we as Republicans believe in, i.e., our basic trust in the free market economy. How could we vote for more government and less freedom by allowing this to occur?

> "Duty is ours, outcomes belong to God. We have fought the good fight. Now we need to finish the race and make sure that posterity and the American people know there were conservatives who opposed the leviathan state in this dark hour." — Rep. Mike Pence, Indiana (now Governor of Indiana)

Economic freedom means the freedom to succeed and the freedom to fail.

"I have doubts that the $750 billion bailout if enacted, would work."
— William M. Isaac, former FDIC Chairman

Notes and Questions: The Bill is Not Paid For "The Paulson Predicament" and flaws in the proposed legislation

Q: What if this does not work with a $700 billion bailout—considering Freddie and Fannie have $1.5 trillion in bad loans!

Q: How can $750 billion prop up $600 trillion in derivatives?

More Troubling Secrets of the Bailout Bill

1. Why didn't the vote of October 26, 2005 HR 1461 "Federal Housing Finance Reform Act of 2005," which I supported, not work? A new board FHFA that will have supervisory and regulatory authority of Fannie Mae and Freddie Mac?

2. Negotiations for this bill included the following persons:
   - Senator Chris Dodd (Banking Committee Chairman)
   - Rep. Barney Frank (Banking Committee Chairman)
   - Sen. Judd Gregg (Republican Ranking Member on Budget Committee Chairman)
   - Sec. Paulson (Secretary of Treasury)
   - (Senator Shelby walked out on the proposal, and he is the Republican Ranking Member of Banking Committee)
   - Rep. Roy Blunt (Republican Whip)
   - Sen. Harry Reid of Nevada (Majority Leader)
   - Speaker Pelosi, Democrat

3. *So, only three members of the House of Representatives and Secretary of Treasury—why? Under the Constitution, all money is appropriated in the House. Where were the Chairman of the Appropriations Committee and the Republican Minority Leader in the House?*

4. $5 trillion of loans, of which $1.5 trillion are considered pretty bad and nonperforming from Freddie and Fannie debts.

Conclusion: Paulson had a conflict of interest as the former CEO of Goldman Sachs, where the year prior they cornered the subprime security mortgage market and made $4 billion in profit. His firm, together with Bear Stearns, created these toxic securities. He has a conflict of interest and is simply trying to bail out Wall Street. His initial request was *un-American*. Paulson has asked for no review, no judicial review, no congressional accountability. He is advocating a centralization of power that is totally un-American. Gingrich said he would probably vote for the plan because there was no choice. Grrr … Ugh … *There was a choice.*

Bailouts: Keynesian Solution

With the recent bailouts in Congress, Americans are wondering if capitalism works and when the next bust is going to happen. Having voted against the TARP for Wall Street and the huge stimulus package, I am wondering the same thing. Do we have to deflate our money every time there is a crisis, with the Federal Reserve stepping in by printing huge sums of money and transferring it to the Treasury Department, where they hand it out to businesses that they deem important and necessary? Congress has no say so on this matter once the bill is passed. There are rarely any safeguards with the legislation, and complete carte blanche authority is given to these two government agencies, which is *downright* awful. *Mr. Paulson changed his strategy from buying the toxic loans to bailing out Wall Street firms and banks.* The ten largest banks that received the money were the same banks that purchased credit default swaps and made money off the sale on packaging of these financial devices. They get bailed out because they are considered "too big to fail."

Rubbish.

But what is the pretext for these bailouts? It is Keynesian economics. His mantra of "but we only owe it to ourselves!" is the password for all economic theory. We did it in every major financial crisis in America and England also. The government becomes GOD. Keynes's ideas have become the basis for socialistic governments around the world. To get the economy moving again, Keynes taught, it was the responsibility of government to create full employment, even if it had to borrow money and assume huge debt to do so. Rather than get rid of the problems that created the economic depression—greed, corruption and incompetence—and then allowing the markets to work and punish those folks who caused the problems, these folks get bailed out. Why? Because of Keynesian economics and political might. Those at the levers of power are generally connected to Wall Street or big financial institutions. Again, contrary to basic business logic.

Excessive government spending and mounting public debt appear to provide some good in the short term. But in the long term, Keynesian economics only make things worse and create grounds for the inevitable collapse of the country again. Keynes had a flippant answer for this: "In the long term, we are all dead."

In all my twenty-four years in Congress, we have never seriously tried to reduce debt or reduce the deficit even under Republican control. Yet this colossal public debt is hurting our sovereignty and will eventually move us to a one-world government. Even with the TARP bailout, we had to bail out Chinese banks and European banks. Globalism creates interdependence, which creates a crisis everywhere. Is it the responsibility of the government to prime the economic pump? What is good for a family surely must be good for a nation. What would a family do in an economic crisis? Just the opposite to what Congress and the Administration did.

A responsible family would reduce spending and become more productive. They would not take on more debt. And they would look for other ways to not just save money but also increase the revenue to the family. Take another job or become more efficient—and on a national level, if there was incompetence or corruption involved, put some folks in jail and or allow the businesses to go bankrupt. Do not reward bad business decisions. But we have done just that with these bailouts. Giving money to financial institutions that created the problems with no supervision or controls. As the Inspector General (IG) for the Treasury Department recently reported, half of the money given out was unaccounted for, and there were cases of corruption. The government spends taxpayers' money to do what they think is in the best interest of those in power. A sad commentary.

So what is Keynesian *economics? Simply* put, it is the assertion that the government has all the answers! It can create something out of nothing—prosperity. Or said another way, the government is God. That is Keynesian economics. And how do we solve the mounting debt we build up to cover the deficit stimulus spending? By rising population and controlled inflation, they say. Abortion is legal in America, and therefore, we cannot count on the rise of population. Regarding inflation, few management systems, including dictatorships, have been able to control inflation. So where will the money come from to pay this debt? To make the borrowing possible, all nations will be tied together to create a world bank to set up an international economic construct. Keynesian economics has put this construct together so that, in the very near future, we will have international control of our banking system.

So what is the alternative solution?

Yes, there is a predictive business cycle already built into the economy. Also, there were factors that could pull an economy upward from depression and recessions by itself. During these times, savings would rise, and therefore, interest rates would fall, making money available for industry to expand, thereby helping to create jobs. The economy would slowly rise and, with it, interest rates, which would cause the economy to eventually weaken. So the cycle would continue.

Keynes did not believe this would work and thought that a nation could remain in a depression. He said that, at the bottom of the business cycle, there would be no savings to reduce interest rates and cause the cycle to move up again. The static values of savings and investment would not work. The business investment and enterprise could not be dependable. There was no constant guarantee of an upward movement of the economy. He believed there needed to be a tonic, a catalyst, to get the economy moving again. That tonic was planned government investment.

Does a family need that to pull themselves up? No. So why would a nation?

Keynes created a permanent condition of government borrowing and deficit spending. In fact, that has become the recommended course of action for all nations. People must abandon the insane idea that they can borrow their way out of bankruptcy.

Chapter 8
Ousted and a Fact of Life

During any congressional career, there comes a time when you must either take on one of your colleagues who wants the same position of leadership—or one of your colleagues who wants what you have obtained. That is a fact of life.

This chapter is about one of these incidents. I have seen it occur when an incumbent leadership position is suddenly challenged out of the blue by another member, and for the most part, he usually falls short. In the case of the coup d'état when Gingrich was speaker, it was a formidable *but a* foolish plot to oust the Speaker because of his poor management skills and erratic behavior. It failed, and the consequences, albeit significant, were mainly light. Tom DeLay was not replaced and neither was Dick Armey, both of whom plotted to overthrow Gingrich. The only real casualty was Bill Paxon, who lost his position as leadership deputy during the leadership meetings.

The case that was presented to me was in the 111th Congress and occurred when member Roy Blunt (Missouri—now a United States Senator) stepped down as Whip after serving in that position for six years. He himself attempted to oust John Boehner by running against him and losing by one vote when Dennis Hastert stepped down because of the Rep. Mark Foley scandal.

Although my situation may seem like a lesser case, it symbolically represents what all members will face in their career sooner or later. And in most cases, there is an appropriate way to handle it that probably can be applied in almost all cases. In my case, I was the ranking incumbent subcommittee chairman of the Telecommunications and Internet subcommittee (aka Telecom subcommittee) of the Energy and Commerce full committee. I held this post after fighting off John Shimkus and Joe Barton's attempt to keep me in another subcommittee that I resignedly held for six years. The committee rules said I was eligible to take over the Telecom subcommittee. After a contentious battle, working with my colleagues Fred Upton and Ed Whitfield, we were able to convince Chairman Barton not to let Mr. Shimkus jump over all of us to take the Telecom subcommittee.

I ultimately solved the problem by giving $250,000 to the National Republican Congressional Committee (NRCC). This was to compensate for the amount of money Shimkus had given. Since he was the pitcher on the Congressional Republican baseball team and Joe Barton was the coach, it was absolutely necessary to do so if I was to attain success. We stopped Shimkus from moving over all of us, and we all simply moved up to the open positions and Shimkus got the Oversight subcommittee.

I first got wind of Mr. Blunt's desire—namely that after vacating his position as Minority Whip that he wanted to oust me as subcommittee chairman—in late November. He intended to run for the United States Senate and wanted to use this new position as subcommittee chairman to raise money from the telecommunications and Internet industries' political action committees.

It came to me via K Street [lobbyists], and when Barton called me to say that he was going to look at all members' contributions to the National Republican Congressional Committee (NRCC) to see if they fulfilled their obligations and was going to assign the new subcommittee chairman for all the subcommittees based upon their contributions, their voting records with the full committee, their votes during markups, and their votes with the Republicans on the House floor, I knew something was up. He also wanted to assess how everybody did with their financial obligations for the President's dinner fundraisers that occur twice a year [NRCC biannual party fundraiser]. It was a bit alarming to think that I may not be able to keep my chairmanship after serving twenty years in Congress because of my lack of fundraising for the NRCC. What happened to seniority? Seniority went out the door when Gingrich became Speaker.

Now unfortunately it is all about how much money you raised and were giving out to other members. It was a nightmare of insecurity and angst. Once it was apparent that Blunt wanted my chairmanship, I had to make a plan and convince Barton that I was his man. I also had to convince Leader Boehner. Both he and Blunt had asked for an additional $150,000 from me just before the election in November, and I had deferred because I had already given $250,000. *(The existing culture in both parties required that you freely give to your party these enormous amounts every year.)* They each had come up to me personally and asked for this money. I indirectly refuse and pointed out that I had already given sufficiently and was giving out more of my own money to the candidates in Florida and others I knew who were in trouble. They were not satisfied. Finally Boehner personally came up to me just before the November elections and asked for $100,000 and implied that would be the end of it. I had suggested $50,000, but it was not accepted. So I had a problem with both Blunt, who was using my refusal to take my subcommittee, and Boehner, who was a friend but one who had recently tried (and failed) to shake me down for $100,000. Part of the reason I was pushed for money was that I had a lot of money in my campaign. In fact, I was the leader with the most cash on hand for the Republicans in the House of Representatives. Not because I raised so much money, but because I husbanded my resources, never had a serious campaign, and had very low overhead; I had no consultants and did all my TV campaign ads myself. I also carried my district all the time.

So there I was. Barton, Blunt and Boehner were not dispose to keep me in place. What was I to do? My plan was first of all to compare what my other colleagues did in fundraising efforts for the NRCC, including Barton and also support from other members. They could lobby for me!

I did an excel sheet to show all the members who were subcommittee chairmen and others who were not but were on the Energy and Commerce Committee. Our analysis showed that I was above the norm, meaning that I could not be ousted for failing to do as well as my peers. Of course, Blunt being Whip, had given over $1.5 million, and because of it, he felt he a rightful reason for asking for my slot. I presented this information to Barton. He had his staff also develop his own evaluation, especially based upon fundraising for the president's dinners. I fell down there in that category. Raising money for these dinners is a bit of sham. You ask folks on K Street to give on your behalf. If you get out early, you can get the PACs to give for you. Since I was not a big K Street schmoozer, I never was that successful.

The thrust, therefore, was to show that my voting record on the House floor, and in full committee, was better than that of my colleagues in consideration. Voting mattered didn't it? On this task, we also showed that on key votes I was superior in loyalty, and when I added in the legislation that I sponsored including Energy legislation that Barton developed himself, I was one of his leaders, and in fact, surpassed Blunt.

So I made my case to Barton that, overall, when you looked at my record, including my conservative credentials, which were closer to his than anyone, I should not be ousted. He still was not convinced, and the pressure was building for him to make a decision. I had several other things I felt would help me. The attorney counsel for me in prior years was Dave Cavicke, an outstanding attorney from Stanford Law School who was not only highly intelligent but also politically astute. I had great respect for him and always really treated him with deference because he was so perceptive. I called him and asked that he keep me posted and perhaps put in a good word for me and remind Barton how allowing Blunt to oust a sitting member would hurt committee morale and give Blunt the appearance of trying to be more than greedy.

Cavicke worked behind the scenes to tell Barton how important seniority was and how members who had institutional memory would be discouraged if persons in leadership suddenly came in and took over while others, during the years they were in leadership, were toiling in the fields. Pressure continued to build, and K Street was signaling that they wanted Blunt in a subcommittee chairmanship somewhere. Some of them wanted him to take over Energy, where the big Global

Warming legislation would be developed. That was not good for me because then Fred Upton, who was subcommittee chair of Energy, would want his old Telecommunications Subcommittee back.

So there I was. I had the records showing NRCC support, member voting support, and sponsoring legislation support. There was nothing left to do but lobby K Street and our leadership, and so I proceeded to do just that. K Street friends were ambivalent because of Blunt's former leadership position, and my past experience with leadership was tentative. I had two things going for me. Dave Cavicke and Barton genuinely liked me and saw what a good job I was doing in the past. Plus I had given out over $350,000 from my campaign. My constant humorous and intentionally substantive conversations with Barton were making their mark.

I approached Boehner and asked what it would take to keep my chair and why, with my seniority, I was being subjected to this. I also appealed to the fairness issue and characterized Blunt's move as a power grab by someone who was leaving the House for a Senate run. Boehner was receptive and suggested, again, that I give more money, which I tentatively agreed to once I got the slot and suggested that it would be over the normal cycle. Furthermore, I hinted that the money I had in the bank surely would never go to anyone if I were ousted. At this point I still had more cash on hand than any Republican member in the House.

I still needed a breakthrough to win my case. I told Barton that Boehner was okay with me staying on as chairman. I also advised him that I just hired the fundraising firm Bellwether Consulting—they were doing Senator Martinez's fundraising campaign—and that we would have a Full Committee fundraiser in Disney World. They could do this for me. He seemed impressed, and it gave him the idea that all subcommittee chairmen should do the same. I was making headway.

I finally had the solution. What could Blunt be offered that would give him the prestige and overall working ability to not only save face but give him actual opportunity to use his skills? Why not make him vice-chairman of the Full Committee? That way he could be involved with all the subcommittees and could take on special projects for

Barton and help him out with the Healthcare and Energy legislation that was going to be developed by the Obama Administration/House Democrats. Why limit his expertise to just telecommunications? His background as Whip and ostensible smoothness with members would help us to stick together in offering alternative legislation to combat the Democrats. Barton like the idea and suggested it to Blunt to see if he was interested. The simple fact that Barton was offering this new position showed Blunt that his ousting me was not going to be easy and that Barton was offering him a unique opportunity. Blunt demurred, but the circled had turned. He was on the defensive, and he would have to turn this down when it was really a good position for him and, most importantly, it made sense to Barton.

After several more weeks, the decision had to be made. Barton pressed Blunt, and I continually worked behind the scenes and had a little help from Boehner, who cautioned *Barton not to oust me* without thinking it through. This nudge from Boehner really helped. (Later Blunt admitted this to me after this was over.)

In our final meeting, everyone was asked if they wanted to retain their subcommittee chairmanship. We all said yes, and that left Blunt having to really get aggressive if he *wanted* to oust me, and he was now moving from a position of weakness. He finally acquiesced and accepted the Vice-Chairmanship of the Full Committee on Energy and Commerce, and I remained Chairman of the new Communications, Technology and Internet Subcommittee (formerly the Telecommunications and Internet subcommittee aka Telecom subcommittee).

That evening in the cloakroom, Boehner came up to me and whispered in my ear. "You are really, really lucky, lucky."

Chapter 9
Publicity and Sound Bites

Every member wants his voice to be heard. Name recognition is important, and it must be positive. The trick is pursuing it without looking like an opportunist. One of the neat ways to get press is to offer to write an op-ed for your local newspaper on a current topic. You can take the tack that you do not agree with the local editorial board, arguing that it does not have access to the same level of information as you do, and ask for the opportunity to provide an informed counterpoint to their opinion. And you pick a topic that most of your voters would agree with. In my case, I did an op-ed on offshore drilling at a distance of one hundred miles off the coast of Florida.[16] The *Orlando Sentinel* was against it, but the polls showed that most people in my district were for it. Free press at the *Sentinel*'s expense, plus I gained support and credibility.

At committee hearing, you can garner a lot of press by thinking before the hearing about the sound bite you want the public to read. There is an art to finding a metaphor or allegory that is just right for the moment. For example, the press seems to like the expression, "there has been a sea change in opinion on this matter" –or– "this is another Enron loophole for big business" –or– "what did he know and when did he know it?" A good reading of history and literature helps to plant the analogy or metaphor into the listener's mind. "This is the captain of the Titanic and all is well, we just glanced off an iceberg …" Others might be:

- Today we have a magic moment in our history and it could well be the turning point …

- It is not midnight in America but it is morning.

- Make my Day.

- Tax cuts for the wealthy. The rich get richer and the poor get poorer.

- The shadow of the future.[17]

There are many sound bites from sports and movies that would be apropos as well. The best ones are the ones that incorporate the theme of the hearing or subject, putting things into historical context so the listener and the press can get it instantaneously. That is particularly important for the voters to grasp quickly and to identify you with this meaning. Sometimes you can become a national celebrity with just the right sound bite, albeit your notoriety won't last long because there is always another train with a new agenda. The public has a short memory, and you will be forgotten until your next sound bite.

But it can work another way also if you mangle or misspeak or make a callous or inappropriate statement, especially if it has a darker or sexual meaning. You will suddenly find yourself backtracking and wishing you had not said that. Just ask Sen. George Allen about his comment, on video, at a rally in Virginia. He lost his chance to be a contender for President as well as losing his Senatorial election.

Going on national television and radio is also helpful in getting your name out to the public. You have to catch just the moment, however; preferably opportunities that have escaped the notice of others, for example, if you see something happening in the news which is a case of injustice or calamity or simply out of the norm. Imagine you are home for the Fourth of July—along with other members—and you see that President Bush has Secretary of State Condoleezza Rice meeting with the Saudi Arabia Kingdom and offering support for the building of nuclear reactors. Maybe it is good policy to help them and thereby control their development of nuclear energy; however, the United

States is, at the same time, criticizing Iran for doing the same with the help of Russia. Saudi Arabia has the largest desert in the world, with plenty of sun and wind. Why don't they develop that? You could put out a press release and quickly be on every news channel in America. Most people would agree with you, and at the same time, you would be working off the low approval rating of the Executive Branch. The President does it all the time, making Congress the scapegoat for policy decisions, e.g., "Congress spends too much money and has too many earmarks."

You would be on national news and make a name for yourself as a tough-talking member who points out the obvious. Sometimes you want to take a crusade against something or someone who the public knows is wrong or in error, like Congressman Nixon did with the Alger Hiss case. With the help of a whistleblower like Whittaker Chambers, he was able to use that success to become a United States Senator.

All the while, you are sending out daily press releases with your accomplishments and hoping that the press picks it up—or at the very least, the weeklies. What is amazing is that the crowd is not stupid. What happens is that the opinion developed becomes an appraisal of your efforts and your reputation. The book *Wisdom of Crowds* suggests that, after a while, this becomes an acute factor, and you become a statesman or an individual with a persona. Conversely, you can end up like Vice President Quayle and be thought of as stupid and silly—he really wasn't, but his persona became forged by his missteps.

And lastly, newsletters, town meetings, tele-town meetings, and having a spectacular website also help to get your name out.

Over time, these means of communications incrementally build your name recognition and tell people who you are. Many members are now sending out emails every month from lists that can be purchased using the Congressional Clerk Hire Funds, which provides a yearly budget for franking or mailing for every member. When these folks answer you, you then put them into your computer, and you can start communicating with them every month via email newsletter. Answering your mail is so important and necessary to win every two years. Senators do not have to be so conscientious because they get elected every six years, and most of their constituents forget that they did not get a reply and simply see their Senator on TV.

Your fundraising efforts can also tie into your name recognition when you bring down the President, Vice President, Cabinet Officials or the Speaker or leader of your party. These all go hand in hand towards establishing your persona and your ability to influence and ward off opponents.

If ever you are able to get an earmark—or what I like to call a district funding request completion—then you can go around the district and present these checks in the form of large cardboard facsimiles and garner much press also. But you have to be careful not to have your fundraising efforts tie to these earmarks, or you will end up like Senator Stevens of Alaska with his earmark for the "Bridge to Nowhere."

Chapter 10
Freedom and Restraint

Three thoughts on freedom after reading *Alaska Light* by Kim Heacox,[18] which goes to the crux of what freedom really means:

1. When you have freedom you have choice. Choice, in life, gives one the ability to act like God, i.e. you can make moral decisions for yourself and others. You accept moral responsibility and become godlike. This is the possibility God gives you, and by doing so you are closer to God and ultimate salvation.

2. God gives us freedom by divine covenants and not lawlessness (see Galatians, the last two chapters). This is the ultimate democracy where you do not need a government—or very little government—because men and woman do what is right. That is what Walt Whitman was talking about in "Democratic Vistas."[19]

3. Our ultimate survival as a race is dependent on self-imposed restraints more than our freedoms. Be like the wren.

Notable quotations *from this book:*

> "How long will it remain so … I suspect the future of Alaska, even the future of the Earth and ourselves, will be a measure of our own self-imposed restraints more than our *freedoms*? A man can get more easily drunk on freedom than he can get sober on restraint."[20]

"My friends and I prefer the wisdom of the winter wren: an elegant, concise, sustainable economy dedicated to making a living, not a killing."[21]

"I was happy in the immediate process of nature in its most staggering grandeur, in living intimately with something so splendidly immense."[22]

"John Muir came to Alaska looking for glaciers. In late 1800s … on walking on glaciers he said, 'No right way is easy in this rough world. We must risk our lives in order to save them.'"[23]

"It is seldom an altogether easy life in Alaska. People talk about cheating death, but accident rates here are among the highest in the United States."[24]

"Alaska is larger than Texas, California, and Montana combined."[25]

II
Lessons Learned from Legislating

Chapter 11
Scandals, Ethics, and the War-Lost Majority

In *November* 2006, the Republicans lost majority control of the House. You can't help but wonder if it would have helped for Bush to have articulated a better message on why we were in Iraq. The answer I think is yes and no. There was more going on than just that. The Mark Foley scandal could have been prevented if Speaker Hastert had been prudent. He appointed an acknowledged homosexual member from Arizona, Jim Kolbe, to Chair the Page Board, which oversees the House Page program. The Chief Administrative Officer (CAO) also served on the board and was an acknowledged homosexual. Surely he knew that. We could have managed the Duke Cunningham and Bob Ney scandals better, but the Foley scandal was too close to the election. We lost a lot of good members. They are listed below, along with some of their thoughts on the loss.

- Rep. Charlie Bass: "My polls showed I was twenty-nine percent ahead in September, but the popular Governor in New Hampshire had a seventy-five percent approval rating. It was not the war, not Foley and ethics. It was a combination of all these things. They voted straight party line, and they can do that in New Hampshire at the polling machine by just pulling one lever.

- Rep. Chris Chocola: "Too tough a district for my voting record."

- Rep. Thelma Drake: "We need to stop these 527s that are coming out of the woodwork." [527s are tax-exempt groups whose goal it is to influence elections.]

- Rep. Katherine Harris: "Karl Rove, the President and Governor Jeb Bush would not only not help me, but worked against me." [She also complained that the mailings by the state party did not include her.]

- Rep. Melissa Hart: "We ran a good campaign, but we couldn't get anything done, and we just got the ticket splitters."

- Rep. J. D. Hayworth: [Others said he lost because he went negative all through his campaign when he should have gone positive at the end.]

- Rep. Nancy Johnson: "They used marketing deceit … we try to answer with a business plan."

- Rep. Anne Northrop: "For twenty-two months, MoveOn.org was phone banking in my district, and the last three months they would picket in front of my home on weekends. It was the war, and there was nothing I could do."

- Rep. E. Clay Shaw Jr.: "The President should have fired Rumsfeld in July and not waited till after the election."

- Rep. Don Sherwood: "I had my problems."

- Rep. Ron Simmons: [Wanted to know who was going to pay for lawyers in his recount.]

- Rep. Charles Taylor: [Just too much negative press.]

- Rep. Curt Weldon: [No support from Republicans and was betrayed.]

Rep. Boehner pointed the way with his comment that we must earn our way back.

"What happened Tuesday were events we can't control. The war in Iraq, the President's low popularity, and corruption charges. We haven't been acting like Republicans."

I liked what Rep. Bill Young of Florida said about his campaigning. He told his opponent three things.

"You run your campaign, and I will run mine; we don't agree on anything, so there is no use in debating; and after this is all over, we will be good friends."

Probably good advice for incumbents with a weak opponent or someone who has no money.

When you look at the scandals, you as a member always have to realize there are five areas of ethical risk that confront you every day.

1. Balancing congressional work with campaign or political work. Just how much these activities can overlap before your behavior is deemed unethical is a grey area—which is why the member needs to carefully manage this at all times. The reality is that a member is operating in an environment where political and official interests will always overlap to some extent.

2. Gifts and travel. There are strict rules and limits governing what you can accept. Often there is a thinly disguised conference, trip, or meeting where individual lobbyists or groups can influence a member. No matter how hard the member may work at these meetings, the member must be always aware of strict adherence to the rules and watch for any appearance of impropriety.

3. Handling campaign contributors—their access and preferential treatment. This is the area of greatest potential risk when it comes to appearance of impropriety questions. Any action involving campaign contributors, particularly those who gave a significant amount, is inherently suspect.

4. Constituent services intervening with the executive branch on behalf of constituents. Going to bat for your constituents is a routine part of your duties. Just how far you can go on their behalf, before you begin to exercise undue influence, is a grey

area and always subject to questions. (Case in point is Governor Bob McDonnell of Virginia.)

5. And last but not least is sexual impropriety. In this area, the final arbiters are the voters. In some districts, much is accepted as a natural occurrence, and as long as the member is apologetic and shows remorse, he can survive. In other districts, it is the kiss of death and defeat. The congressional ethics manual is not about to discuss this behavior in detail, but it is obvious that standard morality is the watchword.

These set of instructions are from *Setting Course: A Congressional Management Guide26* given out to every newly elected member.

When you look at the major scandals, you can see quickly where Duke Cunningham and Bob Ney went wrong. For Cunningham it was mixing campaign contributions with his own personal use and being unduly influenced by lobbyists. With Ney it was intervening on behalf of contributors and outright stealing.

But when it is all said and done, a member must recognize that good ethics frequently conflict with that which is politically expedient, and balancing the two is a complex, sometimes time-consuming process.[27]

Could the Republicans in the majority overcome these occurrences? I think so. Let's take each of the members who lost and hear why they lost. In my interviews with them, it became apparent that Bush should have fired Rumsfeld in July and made his announcement of the surge back then. He should also have defined what success meant in Iraq.

Sure, President Bush spent too much of the taxpayers' money and House Speaker Hastert did not act independently of the Executive Branch. We rubberstamped Bush's emergency appropriations for the war in Iraq. Under President Bush, the House was little more than a presidential stamp or handmaiden. Whether it was the huge farm bill of 2005, or *No Child Left* Behind Act of 2001 (NCLB) of $75 billion, or the Medicare Prescription Drug Program that ballooned from $399 billion to over $600 billion because of either poor estimating or intentional hiding of the facts—there was always a sense that the

Administration was either manipulating the facts or playing politics to get things passed. There was never sense that OMB [Office of Management and Budget] was providing accurate information.

I was shocked one day to hear Hastert indicate that "the primary responsibility [of the House] … was to pass the President's legislative program."[28]

What I never understood is why the President did not make an intellectual case for the war in Iraq. He could repeat in an open press conference what these many terrorists said against our country, namely, Muhammad, Saladin, Khomeini, and bin Laden and current leaders of al-Qaeda. These people do not favor a constitution but a theocracy. Under the Ottoman Empire, they never had a democracy in 1,300 years. The 1916 Anglo-French decision, also know as the Sykes–Picot agreement, in Arabia was, in point of fact, double dealing by the West in their mind's eye. That is why they are upset today.[29]

The Arabs were furious over the partitioning the Ottoman Empire into wholly artificial entities, and that is why they are still upset and complaining today. The Islamists model themselves on the early Islamic conquerors and want to relive and aspire to Allah's Universal Empire.[30]

Why didn't the President explain that to the American people? He could have explained that this is what we are up against—that they love death as much as we love freedom and life.[31] They want to abolish human laws and implement their Sharia Law. It is the old Manichean struggle.

Could the President have subtly made the argument that we could have victory in Iraq and that this was indeed a clash of civilizations? Take the book *The Victory of Reason: How Christianity Led to Freedom, Capitalism and Western Success* by Rodney Stark.[32] He could have talked in a nuanced fashion about the need for success and how, regardless of our mistakes, we should push forward to victory. The surge in Iraq eventually accomplished this victory.

I guess it would have been politically incorrect for the President to say this publicly.

The money we are spending in Iraq ($12 billion a month) is unacceptable. Because of the 1916 agreement, they want the land back. If they have four wives and embrace death, what are we to do?

Even after the UN resolutions gave us the opportunity to invade Iraq, we could have, at least, had an exit strategy. *Notwithstanding* the mistakes, the President had an obligation to explain to the American people what the real costs were and not continue to mask or trivialize them. His job was to provide an alternative message of an exit strategy, just like Nixon did in his campaign for President after Johnson left office. Timeline it, establish what the definition of success is: I asked that in a closed door meeting with the Ambassador to Iraq, Joint Chief of Staff of the Military, General Petraeus and John Negroponte. One measure of success I was hoping for was that the Iraqi people have more oil production today than under Saddam. Not at that time. *Their answer was unintelligible.*

Also, have we explained the value of a democracy to the Iraqi people well enough? Free will is a necessity of nature in mankind. For this reason, a Sharia theocracy won't work. Islam uses state government as an end, not a means. Totally contrary to what we believe.

Chapter 12
The Budget and Awful Numbers No One Believes

Every year there is a report entitled "Financial Report of the United States Government."

It is the most overlooked report in Washington.

The last credible report was from David Walker, Comptroller General of the United States. He resigned at the end of 2007 because no one took his numbers seriously, including the President, and he started a foundation to educate the public on the enormous debt this country has incurred over the last eight years and before. He is pleading with our citizens to see what is before us, and this is before the new debt from the economic crisis, i.e., the great recession of 2008.

In his last report from December 17, 2007, he presented a grim picture of where we stand. This report alone should have tipped off the investors of this country to the deplorable financial condition this country is in. Let's start with the basics. The federal government does not maintain effective internal control over financial reporting (including safeguarding assets) and obeying the laws and regulations of the country.[33] Mr. Walker did not even have the means to get compliance with these laws. Here is a capsule listing of his findings. (There were only 3,000 copies of this report, and no members of Congress received it except the majority and minority leaders of both parties.)

Walker states that (1) there are serious financial management problems at Department of Defense. (2) Federal government demonstrates an inability to adequately account for and reconcile intra-governmental activity and balances between all agencies of government. And (3) the federal government is totally unable to prepare consolidated financial statements.

As he states in his report:

> "Until the problems outlined in our audit report are adequately addressed, they will continue to have adverse implications for the federal government and the American taxpayers."

Amen. He could, however, provide an adequate and accurate opinion on the 2007 Statement on Social Security, which was only the second year in which it has been presented as an accurate assessment of where we are. Heretofore Social Security was not presented as a basic financial statement. Now read what his assessment is:

"This statement shows that projected scheduled benefits exceed earmarked revenues by approximately $41 trillion in present value terms for the next 75-year period."[34]

What is even more alarming is that the federal government's fiscal exposures totaled approximately $53 trillion as of September 30, 2007, up more than $2 trillion from a year before. But just as important is that there was an increase of more than $32 trillion from about $20 trillion as of September 30, 2000. So even without Obama's new spending, just under Bush, the federal government, according to the Comptroller General, increased our total debt about two and half times from where it was in 2000—an unbelievable increase under a Republican President's watch. This translates into a current burden of about $175,000 per American, or about $455,000 per American household. Where was the press when this report came out, and why didn't they ask the President about these alarming increases?

Secretary Henry Paulson, Jr. signed the 2008 Financial Report of the United States that was presented in September 2008. It was not as illuminating nor as transparent as Mr. Walker's report, especially from a historical sense. His letter in the report did admit that the government's net operating cost for the fiscal year that ended September 30, 2008, was just over $1 trillion, more than triple the net operating cost for the prior year. Yes it was in part due to the economic downturn. Even Paulson said we have an unsustainable fiscal path but was not as specific as Walker was in his letter to the President, President of Senate (VP Cheney) and the Speaker of the House.

Now, there are those who say we can get this under control or that the debt, as a percent of our GDP, will improve as our economy again takes off. But when it does, my experience indicates that Congress will spend more money, and we will not balance the budget. Debt will just increase unless we have the will to stop it. I do not see this will today.

There is a budget committee in both the House and the Senate. The President submits his budget, but generally it is only used as a guide. Under the Bush administration, like all others, it was dead on arrival—even when the President's party is in control of both the Senate and the House. The appropriators carefully guard their jurisdiction and do not let the budget committees of Congress or the President decide what the final budget will be. It is in the Constitution that they are in charge. That is why the subcommittee Chairmen are called Cardinals. The process is totally flawed and does not work. And it is too powerful and biased.

When we try to reduce the spending on this Appropriations Committee, we always fail, and all the appropriators vote to spend *whatever* they deem necessary. Again, they believe it their constitutional right. It is so frustrating for a senior member of Congress to see it happen every budget cycle. Also, we almost never get the budget voted in the House on time, i.e., before the fiscal year ends and, for the most part, it becomes a temporary continuing resolution (CR), which is subsequently voted on in the middle of the night as an omnibus-spending package. Very few members of Congress know what is contained in the final bill. It is an absolute shame. Surely, in a democracy, you should see what is in the final bill. But it rarely happens. In the last ten years, we have had a CR and the final appropriations bill occurred in the following fiscal year as an omnibus-spending bill that no one ever saw before voting. It is never shown to members except perhaps twelve hours before we vote, even when the rules say otherwise.

We need an outside commission like the BRAC Commission [Base Realignment and Closure] used for shutting down military bases to eliminate federal programs and to hold spending down. I know members of Congress have this responsibility, but they have relinquished their responsibility again and again because of the process and power of the Appropriations Committee in the House. We have had votes to cut the federal budget by two percent across the board, then one percent, and both of these motions failed (I offered these cuts on the House floor). Surely you can cut a federal budget by one percent! And in the middle of a recession (possible depression), the Obama administration pushed and passed, with Democrat majority support, an increase of eight percent over the last years in discretionary spending. And more recently in the DOD Budget, it was increased by thirteen percent for FY2009. Previous bills were increased by as much as twenty percent—simply outrageous considering inflation was zero percent.

Why? With an economic downturn and inflation at less than three percent, why push a spending bill that is almost three times inflation? The budget process is flawed, and unless we can get it under control, we will not have a republic, much less a country. Inflation will either destroy us, or we will go bankrupt. That is why David Walker quit as comptroller and is touring the country to tell the American people of the grave danger that we face. He is a worthy American, and we should listen to him before it is too late.

Chapter 13
The Speaker Dennis Hastert

The Speaker of the House is third in line to the President after the Vice President. So it is an important position and ultimately can be just as important as the President if he or she views their position correctly. They are to be independent of the executive branch, not a rubber stamp, even when the President is of the same political affiliation. With the meltdown of our economy and the huge number of people that are out of work and the loss of savings by the American people, the question is asked: Could the Speaker have made a difference, and if so, why didn't he?

I believe this is a fair question. President Bush was recently listed by *Time* magazine as one of the persons who caused this meltdown. Surely Speaker Hastert also shares some blame. Why do I say that? Because he took the jurisdiction of the U.S. Securities and Exchange Commission away from the Energy Commerce Committee where it had resided for over forty years and gave it to the Financial Institutions Committee, which was formerly the Banking Committee. He also took what is called the FASB (Financial Accounting Standards Board) jurisdiction away from the Energy Commerce and also gave its jurisdiction to the former Banking Committee. Now why was that a problem (and how, you might well ask, should I know)?

For one, I was Chairman of the Subcommittee on Energy and Commerce that had jurisdiction over the FASB and had a hearing (and more to come) on the Fannie Mae and Freddie Mac illegal hiding of debts by CEO Franklin Raines and other executives so they could get bonuses—including the board of directors, who were paid enormous sums of money. Speaker Hastert took this jurisdiction away from me because of my scheduled hearings. Nothing was done to follow up on these problems on the Banking Committee and the problem became political and died.

I am not saying this change in jurisdiction caused the meltdown, obviously, but it did leave oversight and the aggressive ferreting-out of malfeasance without leadership. Let me set the stage for why this happened and what it meant.

I have been through both the S&L Crisis in the early nineties and the Enron hearings. As an active participant in the Enron hearings, I saw how easy it was to take debt and hide it under what is called "Special Purpose Entities," which were basically sham partnerships that purchased corporate debt to get it off the balance sheets of companies who were trying to push their stock on Wall Street. And as conferee on the Senate/House Committee dealing with final legislation for the S&L crisis, I saw how S&L executives loaned money to developers who were not credit-worthy.

This is something that happens in the housing/real-estate market. In a free, capitalistic market there have to be controls and oversight. Otherwise, shysters will take advantage of the public, and too often, public greed will allow it to happen. Ayn Rand might think that we need no governors, but from my experience, there has to be oversight, regulations and controls to establish security in the market. You have but to read *Extraordinary Popular Delusions & the Madness of Crowds*[35] by Charles Mackay to understand why. The public is so unsophisticated when it comes to investing that human greed oftentimes overpowers rational thoughts. Just read Ben Jonson's play *The Alchemist*.[36]

So what we have is the combination of factors. First, separating the jurisdiction on the Securities industry and FASB and giving to a committee that has no experience with this, oversight which basically prevents real oversight –and– second, making the decision for the chairmanship on the basis of a compromise with Rep. Michael Oxley of Ohio and Rep. Billy Tauzin of Louisiana, which created the division of oversight into these two committees. This division set up a huge round of campaign finance obligations by both Tauzin and Oxley that prevented them from properly getting to the heart of the Fannie Mae and Freddie Mac crisis. And because of this demand for money, these two committees catered to K Street and kept helping them rather than the American people with strict oversight. And the ultimate problem came when Republicans lost their majority and the liberal Barney Frank, who always protected these government entities, together with the liberals already on the committee ... well, you had lack of oversight, in the wrong committee, and the money game causing members to look the other way.

A third factor, too, was in play. Because of this division and the money game, the member from Louisiana, Richard Baker, never got an opportunity to get his reform bill dealing with Freddie Mac and Fannie Mae to the House floor. The steering committee did not select him to become minority-ranking member on this committee, which was a shame, considering the expertise and the ability he had to bring these GSEs [government-sponsored enterprises] to heel.

All of this happened on Hastert's watch, and again, his entire modus operandi involved doing whatever President Bush wanted, rather than what was right—or at least give the House its independence to determine the difference. They could have passed a reform bill dealing with Freddie Mac and Fannie Mae, they could have stopped the pork barreling, and also done much more oversight on the war. But he did not have it in him.

In fact, the number of pork-barrel projects went from 550 a year to 14,000 under Hastert's watch. As pointed out in many newspaper articles and websites, he got himself a huge funding request near to his own property wherein he was able to sell off part of the land to a developer and make millions. He had Bush come into the district to dedicate this new expressway that was within two miles of his property.

All of this is being borne out by the recent story that Freddie Mac is investigating itself over a $2 million lobby campaign to prevent Congress from instituting laws to curbs its unlawful hiding of its debt off its books. The internal investigation is happening even as the

Obama administration provides $200 billion more in government assistance to Freddie Mac and its larger sister-company, Fannie Mae. These two government-sponsored enterprises are the largest providers of home mortgages in America. They secretly hired Republican consulting firm DCI Group of Washington to stop a proposal in the Senate in 2005 sponsored by Sen. Chuck Hagel, R-Neb. The DCI Group did not file lobbying reports describing the work it was performing. They targeted seventeen Republican Senators in thirteen states working to defeat Hagel's bill. The measure was never brought to a vote and died.

A similar action also occurred in the House and was used, I am convinced, to deter Chairman Oxley from offering Richard Baker's bill. I talked to Richard several times as to why his bill was not on the House floor, and he indicated that Oxley was not in favor of it. There evidently were fifty-two outside lobbying firms and political consultants in 2006,[37] which amounted to $11.7 million to prevent a bill coming to either Senate or House floor.

So Freddie Mac made illegal campaign contributions and settled the matter by paying a record $3.8 million fines imposed by the Federal Election Commission in 2006. This does not take into account the twenty lawsuits that were settle by the company because the company fraudulently inflated the price of its stock from 1999 to 2002. The real question is how could this happen, and what could have been done to stop it? And more importantly, how can we prevent this from happening again?

The nexus between money and politics is always there, no matter what. But all of this would change if we limited money spent on campaigns. Take the Oscar nominations as a case in point. No amount of money or advertising could compete with the basic message of the movie *Slumdog Millionaire*. Its basic premise of a poor boy overcoming all the vicissitudes of life and achieving success in spite of the adversities is a perfect case in point. Look up all the other films and their qualifications. Message is paramount, and in politics, policy should be better than money. This movie showed that to be true. So to prevent the constant creep of corruption in our political bodies, we need to limit campaign financing and allow the policy to be the message and operate our campaigns the way Canada and England does theirs. We do not need to spend $13 million on a Congressional seat. The voters can decide without all this money being spent.

If we do that, then the incumbents and challengers will not be persuaded by this huge influx of money, and politicians can go back to what they should be doing, i.e., addressing the people's business in an ethical way rather than pandering to PAC's lobbyists in order to satisfy Senatorial and Congressional committees and build up their own campaign funds. If this does not change, then our country will have scandal after scandal, and eventually our country will collapse.

Dennis Hastert did not see that and fell into the go-along-to-get-along mentality during the most critical expansion of bad credit in America. This also contributed to what caused the American meltdown. Hastert, in retrospect, being from Illinois, with the Blagojevich scandal and its rich stew of corruption, was a product of that environment—whether it was Tony Rezko or William Cellini, who both were indicted for campaign corruption.

"That same year former *Sen. Peter Fitzgerald (R-IL) [The first Republican Senator from Illinois in 20 years]* labeled an Illinois congressional delegation "wish list" of $600 million in projects *that* was submitted to President Bush: a "mega-hog letter."[38]

There was a so-called "combine" in Illinois that continued even under Obama and Secretary of Transportation LaHood *(he was a Republican Congressman from Illinois who endorsed Obama)*. Republicans did not have a change with Hastert as Speaker. He was willing to go along to get along.

Chapter 14
American Exceptionalism

> Ronald Reagan was proud to be an American. How 'bout that in a President for a change? We've got instead today, we've got our first post-American President in Barack Obama. He's above all that patriotism stuff. He doesn't believe in American exceptionalism. He says he does, but he doesn't ...
>
> –Former U.S. Ambassador John Bolton speaking at an NRA Convention, April 2012.

The United States of America is unique among the nations of the world. Our history and national character sets us apart. This nation emerged from a concept of liberty—it was formed not by man but by the ideals of man.

Louis XIV of France famously stated, "I am the state." Look throughout world history, and you will see nations and empires created through the ambitions of man. Alexander the Great, Julius Caesar, Napoleon, all built nations with themselves at the center.

Just consider the founders of this nation, all accomplished individuals who placed their country above their personal aspirations. This is, perhaps, most clearly seen in George Washington.

Our independence was wrestled from the superpower of that age, the British Empire, which spanned the globe. Although Washington experienced some successes, the defeats far outnumbered his triumphs. Yet his iron will and determination held together a ragged army that persevered to final victory.

Throughout the annals of history, such successful generals seized the reins of power as their right. And George Washington? After defeating the British, he merely sought retirement at Mount Vernon to enjoy his home and family. This is American exceptionalism—yielding ultimate power to an elected government.

In addition to our country's unique civic heritage, many see a divine element in American exceptionalism. I believe that God bestowed upon our nation a special role in guiding world events.

With the British evacuation of Boston in March of 1776, the conflict shifted from New England to New York. Several days later, John Witherspoon, the president of Princeton University, delivered a sermon that was published as "The Dominion of *Providence over* the Passions of Men."

He sought to show the role of God's Providence in world history or, as the Bible said, "not a sparrow falls but God knows it" (Matt. 10:29). In so many words, he spoke of the divine destiny and exceptionalism of America's role.

He went on to say that the rebellion was part of God's divine plan. He also pointed out that, contrary to history, where political and religious issues were separate, in America they were inseparable. Or as he said from the pulpit, "There is not a single instance in history in which civil liberty was lost and religious liberty kept." This sermon mobilized the fervor of the Revolution and convinced the Americans of their providential need to succeed. So from the beginning, there was a sense that America would be different from all other countries in world history.

As Ronald Reagan so aptly put it in his 1988 farewell address: "The past few days when I've been at that window upstairs, I've thought a bit of the 'shining city upon a hill.' The phrase comes from John Winthrop, who wrote it to describe the America he imagined."

America is that Shining City on a Hill, a beacon of freedom and decency inspiring a weary world. Yes, America is imperfect, stained with the legacy of slavery and expansionism that devastated Native Americans. Yet we recognized our own deficiencies and corrected them. Again, setting America apart.

This American exceptionalism guides us as we act at home and abroad. However, when you look at the overall changes in the Presidency with the election of Barack Obama, one of the biggest differences with past Presidents is the belief in American exceptionalism.

Mr. Obama really doesn't approach foreign policy and national security in the sense that America is exceptional and has a history demonstrating that status. So in one sense, he could be the most radical President this country has ever had.

Throughout our history, nearly every President believed in the principles that America is an exceptional country, not just because of our Constitution, but also because of our historic mission of spreading freedom and democracy.

The best example of this is when he was recently asked outright: "[Do] you subscribe, as many of your predecessors have, to the school of American exceptionalism that sees America as uniquely qualified to lead the world, or do you have a slightly different philosophy? And if so, would you be able to elaborate on it?"

Mr. Obama's reply was telling.

"I believe in American exceptionalism, just as I suspect that the Brits believe in British exceptionalism and the Greeks believe in Greek exceptionalism …"[39]

He really is, as Bolton suggests, the first post-American President we have had. He is acting like President of the world writ large or, as has been often suggested, like global community organizer rather than a Commander-in-Chief. In his mind, the U.S. is just another country rather than a force for good in world history.

When you go back and look at WWI and WWII and see the role we played—include Korea, the Balkans, and Desert Storm—in all of these cases, we protected the injured party, brought freedom, and helped restore the country. This is particularly true with the Marshall Plan in Europe after WWII. Then we left those nations, not as a conqueror, but as a liberator. Other nations throughout history did not leave; they tried to put the country under their control.

Now we have to face a crucial decision in Afghanistan. When Afghanistan was fighting Russia, we helped them, but when we won, we left abruptly without letting them get off the floor and establish a stable country. We seriously undermined that country by not helping it.

The strategy that the Bush administration gave to the current administration was what Obama touted in his March 2009 foreign relations speech. Now he is walking away, indicating that he doesn't want to help that country. In fact, he wants to start prosecuting the CIA personnel who were instrumental in helping us to avoid a terrorist attack for eight years.

Everything, in his mind, is from a consensus through negotiation rather than from established, firm principles. Obama recently said he was shocked at the corruption in Kabul. *That is surprising, since he comes from Chicago.*

In looking overseas, Obama is more interested in currying favor with other countries than he is in protecting our national interests. In traveling around the world on his apology tours, he is appealing to anti-American sentiment, not building sound relations. Many of these nations seek to curb American strength and influence.

American weakness, over the long term, will worry many nations more than American strength because, ultimately, our nation is the primary force for freedom and democracy.

Look at how little support he provides Israel. When you look at the Middle East, the Arab states would go along, behind the scenes, for Israel to take out the nuclear capability of Iran. Israel would get a big secret thank-you for destroying Iran's nuclear program. Publicly, the Arab nations would all criticize Israel vociferously and vehemently, but would, at the same time, expect Israel to continue to prevent Iran from exercising regional hegemony in the Middle East with its potential nuclear capability.

If we hope to return to the majority, Republicans should go back and read the speech made by Ronald Reagan in November of 1979 wherein he announced his candidacy.

"But there remains the greatness of our people, our capacity for dreaming up fantastic deeds and bringing them off to the surprise of an unbelieving world. When Washington's men were freezing at Valley Forge, Tom Paine told his fellow Americans: 'We have it in our power to begin the world over again,' we still have that power. ...

We who are privileged to be Americans have had a rendezvous with destiny since the moment in 1630 when John Winthrop, standing on the deck of the tiny Arbella off the coast of Massachusetts, told the little band of Pilgrims, 'We shall be a city upon a hill. The eyes of all people are upon us so that if we shall deal falsely with our God in this work we have undertaken and so cause Him to withdraw His present help from us, we shall be made a story and a byword throughout the world.'

A troubled and afflicted mankind looks to us, pleading for us to keep our rendezvous with destiny; that we will uphold the principles of self-reliance, self-discipline, morality, and—above all—responsible liberty for every individual that we will become that shining city on a hill."

Without a firm understanding of what makes America exceptional, we become just another country in the UN, basing foreign policy on a consensus.

Presently, we face countless issues around the globe, affecting long-term freedom, independence, and the sanctity of all human life. This is a time that demands American exceptionalism.

Chapter 15
Opportunity

What This Debate is All About

There is probably no ideal that stirs the American heart as much as freedom.

"Don't tread on me." The archetype of the heroic individual who fights for freedom against an oppressive institution. The opportunity to decide for oneself either yea or nay.

Now we have a new president and a Democrat majority party (before Republicans won back majority in *November 2010*) using a crisis to propagate all the socialistic projects that they have been yearning for under the guise of a financial crisis. Will we become like France and be forced to bow to *étatism* [state control/socialism]? Move in that direction and capital and jobs will flee. The Democrats want to socialize healthcare. They want to create a tax on all hydrocarbons with a cap and trade policy. And they want to provide even greater control of education from Washington.

But why is everyone seeking America? Not for the nanny state but for the state of boundless opportunities. All of this will be lost if we do not let the markets work. "Bankruptcy is not the same as liquidation. Save the zombies and you sabotage the vital."[40] Without risk, creativity withers. Without failure, the culture of risk fades. The country's remarkable capacity for innovation, for reinvention, is tied to its acceptance of failure. Churn is the American way. Companies rise and fall, and others come along to replace them. For all of these reasons, we must steer clear of the French temptation.

There will be hurt for those who displayed greed and foolishness. But "the man who works, he votes, generally prays—but always pays"[41] and will not be forgotten. We have a duty to respect that man and not throw the country over the cliff for the reckless ones by accumulating all this debt, a policy of government intervention and permanent statism. We must respect this forgotten man when we seek to solve this financial crisis.

The word "binge" is from the Latin word which means to inflate *and soak*. Obama's plan does not help productivity and ultimately erodes property rights. *Animal Farm* is upon us. The experiment of *Casa Grande's* collective farm in Arizona during the 1930s was tried and failed.

We are a strong nation. The Democrats continue to create a sense of fear-itself, of panic to develop the "Big Bang" agenda to federalize and/or socialize healthcare, education, and energy—the "Commanding Heights" of post-industrial society. This is the most radical agenda of social transformation seen in our lifetime—maybe in all of American history.

Republicans must now offer an alternative vision of how this economy should work and grow. To talk about the living world of the real economy of free trade, competition, entrepreneurship and profit. Milton Friedman's *Free to Choose* is our paradigm. Conservatives have proven ideas and it hinges on a private economy and risk. Under Obama "hope is on hold."[42] Let hope be rewarded with opportunity. Obama needs to be reminded of his own words, "For as much as government can do and must do, it is ultimately the faith and determination of the American people upon which this nation relies."[43] Nothing is too big to fail with hope, determination, and the faith of the people.

Chapter 16
Who Are You?

Once they are elected, most members have no idea how to run things. They have been either attorneys or politicians in a small office or perhaps small businessmen like myself. Even so, they have no idea what the nexus of politics has to do with a normal everyday job, or how to represent their constituents, or go about trying to get things done. Not to mention juggling all of that with raising money from their friends and getting out of debt.

In Washington DC, there are literally thousands of staffers. All of them are very ambitious and not necessarily loyal. They are looking for the next rung. In my first term in office, I reduced their COLA [cost of living adjustment] from 6 percent to 2.5 percent and got nothing but epithets by phone for a year. Little did I realize the homogeneity of congressional staffers. To this day, I still get folks who have left the Hill and remember my motion to reduce staff COLAs!

Since politics is mostly about perception, and there is no bottom line beyond getting reelected, a member has to define who he or she is.

"If you know your role or how you fit within the institution and diligently direct your resources in support of that role, you will greatly minimize inefficiency or the unproductive 'tacking' so common in many House and Senate offices."[44]

Five primary roles have been identified that members play in Congress:

1. Legislative Insider

2. Party Insider

3. Citizen Investigator

4. Statesman

5. Outsider

What do these roles mean? You can major in one of these roles or minor in another. You can guide your career by tapping into these roles.

The LEGISLATIVE INSIDER is a member who works through the committee process. As you gain seniority in Congress, this is generally the role you achieve. These folks want to receive national recognition for their accomplishments. To do this, you have to build close ties with your colleagues, using these personal relationships for political ends, building coalitions, using their expertise to negotiate agreements, and cutting deals behind the scenes. Examples of these types are Rep. John Dingell, etc.

These members have a lot of patience, and they know how to use national press to generate support for their legislative activities.

The PARTY INSIDER is a member who wants to promote the power and ideology of their party. These folks want to be party leaders or in positions of leadership within the party. They are team members who want to build up chits to gain access to power. They like ideology and want their party to dominate. They know who is vulnerable and where to go to get money and resources. They also have excellent media and communications skills and excel in spinning the party message to the press and the public. These folks want to move up the national political ladder, either in Congress or in appointed positions in the Executive Branch.

The CITIZEN INVESTIGATOR is a member whose primary focus is acting as champion for local and state interests, but also acts as guardian for the public interests and investigates complaints against the government. Their parochial interests allow them to gain statewide recognition and advance their careers on a state level, e.g., as Governor.

The STATESMAN is a member who views *themself* as serving in Congress in pursuit of what is right for the country, rather than what is politically expedient. They may advocate for specific legislative ends, reforming the process or protecting the institution. They want to promote what is good public policy. They have to be careful that they do not alienate *themselves from* their party or the process.

This type of operation fits the role the public likes: a nonpartisan politician who is trying to do the right thing. They oftentimes hang back on issues and, instead, work the process when it meets their needs where they can act as conscience of the process. They try to speak independently and try to generate a national profile and national attention for their view. A good example of this type of member *is Senator John McCain and former member Rep. Chris Shays (R-CT)*. They do not enjoy the member-to-member "schmoozing" and politicking of the legislative insiders and have little interest in controlling party machinery or taking on the organizational tasks of the party insiders. Oftentimes they do not embrace their leadership or do not spend extensive time forming close ties with dozens of their colleagues. They go directly to the national media and hope the media and press can compel their colleagues in Congress to change direction and address their concerns. These members are not often liked for this reason. The upside for them is that the press gives them lots of publicity and every opportunity to communicate their ideals, unencumbered by politics.

The OUTSIDER is a member who shares many of the statesman's predilections and discomfort with the legislative and political process, but they choose to express themselves more boldly. They are big critics of the system. They want everyone to know they're not part of Washington DC. Consequently, rather than trying to straddle the insider and outsider roles as do the statesmen, they accept and usually embrace being an outsider. Their tactics frequently create resentment within the institution, for they try to influence policymaking by framing the debate through their public rhetoric rather than through the regular legislative process.

Outsiders tend to act impatiently and use tactics that bring attention on themselves and the inefficient operating system. They are risk-takers who steer away from the safe path and are interested in using their positions as a platform to get press. They are not as interested in making laws. They want to be perceived as independent of the system. The danger of this mode of operation is that you can alienate leadership, and you are off the reservation, consequently condemned to a career as an outsider. Former Speaker Newt Gingrich started out as an outsider. As his message of change begin to take hold among House Republicans, he shed the outsider image for that of the party insider and ran successfully for a leadership office. Rep. John Boehner followed a similar path. This path of leadership is an attractive way to avoid paying some of the dues of the conventional path. It is also less risky if you are able to transition into leadership.

Obviously one can take on a major role of the five roles and also play a minor role in others. It will ultimately depend on your personality, the desired mission you set out for yourself and your district and state needs. Your future political plans may play a part in your decision.

"Trying to take on more than two roles—which Members frequently do—can lead to serious problems."[45]

Ultimately, the role a member decides on will require balancing competing interests. The key lies in understanding your own strengths and weakness—as the ancient Greek aphorism suggests, *gnothi seauton* [know thyself]. The difficult challenge facing members is to decide what specialization best suits them. It is also probably wise for veteran members to reassess mid-career to ensure that the role they have chosen makes sense, and if not, develop a new strategy that better suits their needs and goals.

III
Lessons Learned About Democracy

Chapter 17
Recognizing Good Politics and A Bad Bill, Obamacare

SOMETIMES YOU CAN'T MAKE
A BAD BILL BETTER

During the Energy and Commerce Committee markup of the Democrat healthcare (later Affordable Care Act or Obamacare) bill HR 3200 in June 2009, it became apparent early on that none of the Republican amendments would pass and that the chairman of the committee, *Mr. Henry Waxman (D-CA)*, was not going to cooperate with our ranking Republican, Joe *Barton (R-Texas)*. In fact, less than twenty-four hours before the full markup, the Democrats offered a manager's amendment that was a substitute for the already 1,000-plus-page bill they had allowed us to see. So in fact, we were forced to vote on a bill that had been changed so as to get Democrat votes. No one on our committee had read or seen this new bill of 1,067 pages.

During the four-and-a-half-day markup, Republicans offered a host of amendments. Some of them were ruled out of order, and others failed on a partisan vote. Even the amendment that I offered, to ensure that the American consumer could keep his own healthcare after five years if they wanted to, was defeated. Amendments dealing with e-verify for illegal immigrants, a pro-life amendment to ensure taxpayers do not have to pay for abortions except in the case of rape and incest and the life of the mother, a ceiling on overall spending, and the allowance of cooperatives to compete for healthcare all failed. We went to almost midnight during these markups.

We wanted to offer more amendments, but it was agreed that we would come back at a later time to consider these amendments, including another fifty to seventy Democrat amendments that the chairman needed in the bill to garner Democrat support. Subsequently, after the August break and at the end of September 2009, Chairman *Waxman* approached our ranking member Barton about the subject markup. Mr. Barton agreed to the markup, but also agreed to limit our amendments to only amendments that Waxman would agree upon. So in a sense we were going to be allowed certain amendments from the previous markup that were not offered but no new ones. Mr. Barton agreed not knowing what the amendments the Democrats would propose. *Here is the rub and the fallacy from a political standpoint. It is really important to recognize the political situation at hand when you agree to reopen a bill that was already out of our committee and had been reported.*

First of all, House bill HR 3200 was lambasted in the public forum, and our base was strongly against it. Also, the bill was on life support because you could not get the Senate to even consider this bill. There were two bills in the Senate, and at the time of this second markup consideration, there were three bills in the House: one from our committee, one from the Ways and Means Committee, and a third from the Education and Labor Committee. The seniors were against the funding of the bill HR 3200 for taking almost $500 billion from Medicare over ten years. Consider that Medicare was going bankrupt and the doctors were complaining about being underpaid. So what would be the purpose of going back into another markup to get one or two amendments of ours that would make the bill more palpable to conservative Democrats when the fundament direction of the bill was wrong? *But Waxman needed the Blue Dog Democrats if he wanted to pass a bill. He had to include their requests.*

That was the scene when Mr. Barton called the Republicans in for a conference for a second short markup of bill HR 3200. There are twenty-three Republicans on the Energy and Commerce Committee and almost everyone showed up for the meeting just prior to the next-day markup. Mr. Barton outlined the ground rules and the intention to offer a number of amendments that he thought would improve the bill and give us an opportunity to participate in the healthcare debate.

But why do this, considering where we were and the fact that the bill was still on life support?

Mr. Barton wanted Mr. Joe Pitts (PA) to offer his pro-life amendment and a couple of other amendments dealing with tort reform and possibly illegal immigration. All of us in the room knew they would not pass, but the opportunity for the Democrats to open the bill and put in a whole new set of amendments that we had not seen seemed foolish. In fact, the next day we did not see twenty-seven of their amendments because they were offered en bloc, which means they were put all together as one manager's amendment. They were to be offered to the Rules Committee for engrossment in the bill.

When I asked Mr. Waxman how this was done, he could not provide a clear answer except to say it was up *to* the Rules Chairwoman how she would place them in a bill that was already reported out of our committee. Why we were marking up anything after the bill had gone from our committee is still a mystery to me. Evidently the Democrat strategy was to include Democrat amendments to garner votes on the House floor, and this was the only way to do it. Otherwise the individual amendments might not pass on the floor or would be an embarrassment to individual Democrats. If the public saw these amendments, the Democrat who benefited could not get reelected or, if they were not in the bill, he could not vote for the bill. I know that this is how it is done, but in this case the Republicans were in the driver's seat. Mr. Waxman needed us; we did not need him.

During this discussion with Republicans, Mr. Mike Rogers (R-MI) indicated that he had put together a bill that included all the things that the President recently said in this speech on the House floor in speaking to a joint session of Congress. The President wanted the bill to be budget neutral. There was to be no funding for illegal aliens; it was to allow citizens to band together to develop cooperatives to seek private healthcare; allow individual states to come up with tort reform dealing with malpractice suits, and so on. In fact, as the President left the House chamber after his State of the Union speech, I was on the aisle.

I said to him, "Mr. President, why don't you offer your own bill, and we start over with your bill instead of pushing the Waxman bill? The American people agree with what you said tonight."

The President, in his response to me (which I cannot remember verbatim), indicated that we had to work on the bills in Congress to make them better.

He obviously did not know how things work in Congress.

When it was clear that what Mr. Rogers was suggesting was a new bill—and political dynamite because he was going to present it *as the healthcare bill exactly as* outlined by the President, though it would, in fact, be the very same plan outlined by the President in the joint session of Congress—Mr. Barton said we could not do that. He had given his word that no new amendments and/or bills could be offered. When it was pointed out to him that we do not know what the Democrats are offering with their amendments, he indicated that it was his assumption that the Democrat amendments were the ones left over from the markup in June.

I spoke up in favor of offering the Rogers substitute even if it failed because we would have a political statement on what we, as Republicans, believed in rather that voting again against all of the new Democrat amendments. I even suggested that, if Mr. Waxman would not allow us the vote, we could appeal the ruling of the chair. Mr. Barton said he did not want that to occur and, in fact, would side with Mr. Waxman because he had given his word that no new amendments would come up. After much discussion, we finally persuaded Barton to allow Rogers to offer his bill as a substitute, and that we would not appeal the ruling of the chair when it was called out of order and non-germane by Mr. Waxman.

But the politics was set. It became apparent what the point of this meeting was; it was a recognition that, in politics, you have only a few options when you are in the minority and the public is on your side. *Do not try to make a bad bill better, for attempting to do so, in fact, often it makes it worse and does not help it along.* If the fundamental bill is flawed—which this bill was because of the huge cost and the nationalization of America's healthcare at a time when the economy was weak—it should not be doctored to mask the fact. *Plus it allowed political cover for conservative Democrats.* The President did not agree with some of the things in this bill, so why allow the opposing party to open it up again to help their members get their special exemptions in place? Do not try to make it better if the bill is wrong from the start; and above all, be proactive and try to substitute your ideas. Do not let them co-opt your actions by giving them the opportunity to offer your team two or three amendments while they offer their fifty to seventy!

The important point is to recognize when a member such as Mr. Rogers has hit upon a strategy that will open up the debate to our advantage. *Mr. Barton kept saying he had given his word, but his word was wrongly given in the first place, and furthermore, the circumstances had changed for all of us.*

Would he keep his word if it meant that we would all lose an election because this bill brought in more *Democrats* who could now vote for the bill while we got practically nothing? Would he keep his word when he had not seen any of the amendments that Waxman was offering? Would he keep his word when a questionable procedure was used? It was a flawed bill that was already reported out of our committee. Would he allow the majority to insert anything they desire into this bill without our knowing about its content? The simple thing to do was for him to realize his commitment was made before the battleground environment changed. He finally agreed to allow us to offer the Rogers bill. So finally it was offered, and debate was limited. No vote was called, and it was ruled by the Chairman to be out of order.

But the lesson was made to all of us in that room. In the minority, do not try to make a fundamentally flawed bill better. Try to substitute your bill, and do not back off. Let the public know of your position, and do not let leadership undermine an opportunity when the battleground environment has changed. Mr. Rogers was the hero that afternoon. He had the right instincts for that situation. Out of this meeting, a political law was established.

Chapter 18
Impeachment Almost Aborted — Newt Gingrich Behind the Scenes

Shortly after we came back from the election of 1998, we started to hear rumors that the impeachment of President Clinton was almost aborted. This was when I came back after being reelected that fall, and we were settling in for the State of the Union Address by the President on January 22, 1999. We had lost a lot of members, but we were still in the majority—albeit Newt Gingrich was gone, who abruptly resigned after admitting to adultery with a staffer.

In tracking down these rumors, I went to Representative Chip *Pickering (R-MS)*. Several members had told me about this scenario and that, since he was close to Senator Trent Lott *(R-MS)*, he could confirm them. He did so reluctantly but with the same amazement that I felt.

Total disbelief.

The rumors were that Gingrich had called Senator Trent Lott *(then the Majority Leader in the Senate)* and indicated that he did not think the Republicans should go through with the vote for impeachment in the House—rather we should offer a resolution to forgive President Clinton and show that the Republicans were not willing to subject him to this type of action because of a sexual peccadillo. And he said that we would achieve great political capital if we showed our compassion and regard for the public's disfavor for relentlessly pursuing the President.

Gingrich did not think the Senate would impeach him, and it was a great opportunity to show leadership and Christian mercy by not impeaching him but rather passing a resolution of disapproval or censure of his actions, but not going through with the vote on the House floor together with the huge circus atmosphere of a Senate trial, which was most likely not to succeed.

When I heard this, I was upset. Who was he to propose this without bringing it forward to the Republican conference first? He was going to cut a secret deal with Senator Lott, and they would bring it to us after he leaked it to the press. He would look like the giant savior and force all of us to give in through media pressure. It was indeed outrageous. At the time, all members that I talked to were also upset. Most of them were chalking it up as typical Gingrich, pointing out that they were not surprised because the man could not be trusted.

What I found so baffling was that he would do this on his own and take it upon himself to instigate such a profound change of position from almost all of the House Republicans. Unbelievable. Now I understood why there was a coup against him—his actions were not only erratic, his behavior was in many ways pathological and neurotic. I can only imagine what being in leadership meetings with him must have been like—not only tiring but mind-boggling.

Also, one would have to consider where we were at this point. Now, this was after Rep. Henry *Hyde (R-IL), Chairman of the Judiciary Committee*, had endure personal attacks from the Clinton White House—digging up an affair he had almost twenty-five years ago—and the personal attacks on the special prosecutor Ken Starr himself.

I remember that shortly after Starr submitted his resolution for impeachment to the House in November 1998, he was interviewed on ABC's *20/20*. This was Wednesday, November 25, 1998, and it was the first interview he'd given since sending an impeachment referral to Congress in September. In the interview, Starr rejected charges that the case against Clinton was primarily about sex, and that he had acted like a modern-day Puritan in his investigation.

"Lying under oath, and encouraging lies under oath, does go to the very heart and soul of what courts do. And if we say we don't care, let's forget about courts, and we'll just have other ways of figuring out how to handle disputes," he said.

"There is no excuse for perjury—never, never, never," he said. "There is truth, and the truth demands respect."

Although Starr had never been a prosecutor before taking his post as independent counsel, there was a clear consensus from our understanding of the legal process that it was thorough and necessary. In fact, another associate independent counsel, Brett Kavanaugh, said that no one in Starr's office felt the Lewinsky matter should not have been investigated once it came to light.

In light of this, Gingrich's actions were incredible and came with a lot of risk to our base. Many Republicans were convinced that Clinton not only lied but that his actions represented malfeasance in office and that he should be removed on that account. There was enough smoke between Whitewater and the Vincent Foster suicide that we wanted to impeach him. We had enough and could not take Clinton any longer. And then, lo and behold, Gingrich unilaterally tried to engineer things so as to let him go without an impeachment vote or proceedings in the Senate. That would have been just too much.

Fortunately, Senator Lott persuaded Gingrich that he would not go along and, in fact, thought it was a bad idea.

The implications of this initiative is not well known, and perhaps is only important if Gingrich ever decides to run for President of the United States (which of course he later did and lost). Historians will debate and decide if the proposal by Gingrich had validity or would have been politically smart. At the time, as now, I did not think it was, and in fact, I felt it was an affront to the legal process of Ken Starr and Rep. Henry Hyde, the most respected member of the House of Representatives.

Footnote & Lesson Learned

Like Robespierre during the French Revolution, he began his political career as an opponent of capital punishment but later became its leading practitioner and finally lost his own head to "Madame

Guillotine." The founder of Socialism, François-Noël Babeuf, changed his beliefs many times for political reasons, and he was also executed. Gingrich could be put in the same frame of reference with his duplicitous behavior.

Chapter 19
Maintain Republican Control and Majority

With twenty-four years of experience in Congress, I have to ask myself what can be done for my party in order to obtain control of the House of Representatives and keep it after having been in the majority for twelve *years*. Although we did obtain control in *November 2010,* we can lose it again. That is why this observation is so important.

Two things: austerity and simplicity.

Reestablish the simple notion of putting faith in the people. Thomas Jefferson came out of retirement to establish a pure republican form of government with a federal bond among the states; is it possible that is something we should do today, and is it more preferable to what we have to date? Let the states be the innovators on healthcare and civil rights for gays and lesbians and even allow some states to tackle Social Security, Medicare and Medicaid problems with state innovations. Allow them waivers and devolve the federal obligations down to the states.

When Jefferson came out of retirement, his critics, the federalists, thought he was going to dismantle the federal government. In *American Sphinx: The Character of Thomas Jefferson*, historian Joseph Ellis suggests:

> Apart from the natural rights section of the Declaration of Independence, this is probably the most famous political

statement that Jefferson ever made: "But every difference of opinion is not a difference of principle. We have called by different names brethren of the same principle. We are all republicans—we are all federalists."[46]

He was offering conciliation and moderation. For Republicans *to continue to control the* House will mean not a radical break with *Democrat policies* or a dramatic repudiation of the governmental framework established in the Constitution. Jefferson was not advocating the tearing up the government, merely suggesting that the federal bond among the states was preferable to a big overriding federal establishment. This was Jefferson's answer to the federalist position in 1801.

By writing that we are all Americans first he was also saying he believed that with moderation and conciliation we must continue the time-honored tradition of and customs embedded in constitutional law and not tear at the fabric of our nation, but move smoothly towards change. David Hume's *History of England* lays out this approach in the eighteenth century. Hume outlines the spark of constitutional authority that evolved in England. Especially he was talking about the early tradition of self-rule going back to Saxon days at the end of the Roman Empire, when England starting governing itself. This approach fits into the conservative side of governing, which also stresses tradition and custom.

So a wise and frugal government is the platform. Or as Jefferson so ably said in his Inaugural Address (from Ellis again):

> "… a wise and frugal government, which shall restrain men from injuring one another, which shall leave them free to regulate their pursuits of industry and improvement, and shall not take from the mouth of labor the bread it has earned. This is the sum of good government, and this is necessary to close the circle of our felicities."

This was Jefferson's clearest statement of his minimalist theory of government.[47]

In 1801, the national debt stood at $112 million, most of which had accrued as a result of Hamilton's program to assume the state debts."[48] Take this amount and extrapolate it forward to 2008. What do you get? Assume the increase in money supply of about 2.5 percent a year and inflation at around 4.5 percent, and you get a total of depreciated money of 7 percent (money doubles roughly every ten years at this rate) or $146 trillion (Present value =$121 million, Rate per Period=7%, No. Periods=207). Our debt today is $20 trillion. Even if the rate was 5% you would get a $3 trillion debt. How were they going to pay it off?

…..but they did!

This was a staggering sum to this new nation, and yet Jefferson worked to pay it off—and finally did. With his Secretary of Treasury Gallatin's able help, Jefferson was able to cut taxes and retire the debt. As Jefferson later explained to his Secretary of Treasury Albert Gallatin:

"I consider the fortunes of our republic as depending, in an eminent degree, on the extinguishment of the public debt …"[49]

Perhaps the Republicans should make this object their highest priority as well. If Mr. Jefferson were alive today, I certainly think that would be his position. This could be the cornerstone of our national policy. It would be in line with the platform of austerity and could be a God-sent budgetary tool for enforcing this austerity and reducing the size of the government—and also advocating limiting governmental power at the same time.

Would the American people accept a debt-driven fiscal policy? Or would they consider it too extreme? Not if the ramifications were explained to our citizens. History has shown that huge public debt is unmistakably associated with government corruption.[50]

Even when Republicans were in the majority, it could be argued that they were being corrupted. All longstanding political power is inherently corrupt because, as Lord Acton's famous axiom points out, "Absolute power corrupts absolutely."

We had complete control of two branches of government: the White House and Congress. In fact, our majority in the House was almost absolute. Our earmarks exploded under Republican control from 560 a year, when we took over, to over 13,000 a year under the *Chairman of the Appropriation Committee, Bill Young of Florida, and before him Bob Livingston of Louisiana.* From Jefferson to Lincoln to Reagan, the call of America is to be the "world's best hope," or as Lincoln said "its last best hope," or Reagan's "shining city on the hill."

Can we be assured that a republican form of government can exist to ensure national stability without mechanisms of the federal government in all facets of our life? Perhaps it is worth a try. At the very least, we could rely on and emphasize austerity and simplicity with a stripped down version of the federal government and offer more authority and responsibility to the states. That also is what the American Revolution was all about.

We should not need to vote 1,000 times a year and continually change federal laws and create more and more bureaucracies. If we can set the proper course, and we are practicing this approach wisely, we can be assured again in the words of Jefferson that the "forces as natural as the wind and tide … (will) take over and carry America toward its destiny."[51] This must be the Republican faith. And if it was good enough for Jefferson in his day, then surely it must be good enough for us in our day: a positive time-honored Republican platform to again retain and keep the majority in the House of Representatives.

Chapter 20
The Real Shadow Government

Intermingling of Influence between Wall Street, Congress, and Big Business

When I first came to Congress, I thought the entire process was based upon politics, but shortly thereafter, I realized it was all about money. Not just the raising of the money for your campaigns and paying leadership and your party for the right to hold the next tier of leadership, but also when it came to the framing of policy positions. This was and is still a flagrant discrepancy from what I thought our founders intended for this country. Namely, honest debate and pressure to make decisions based upon what is good for the country rather than what was good for a particular interest group.

Yes, I had read the *Federalist Papers* and understood from article 10 that various factions were kept under control in this new democracy by competing against each other and the tradeoff of these groups kept each group intact and prevented the tyranny of the majority. But money contribution and Government-Lobbyist-Influence peddling is rampant and responsible for paralyzing our country so that we cannot make the real changes that are required. What is needed is a strict new code of ethics to stop this influence peddling at the detriment of our country. Congress needs to further define and regulate organized lobbying groups.

But more importantly, Congress needs to put in place a conflict-of-interest test that would prevent business executives coming into the executive branch and not paying capital gains taxes on their portfolios when they do so. This would particularly apply to Wall Street. These folks have the most to gain from having access to the levers of power to promote their previous employer, themselves, or to gain power after they leave working for the government. These folks are either working in government or advising legislators through political action committees so as to help to write legislation and promote their former employers. Sometimes they do not even realize that they have a conflict of interest. They best example of this is the former Secretary of Treasury Hank Paulson, *former CEO of Goldman Sachs.*

The *former* Secretary of Treasury Timothy Geithner is an even more egregious example, having been the New York Federal Reserve Chairman while aiding and abetting AIG and the brokerage houses on Wall Street that benefited from a hundred percent reimbursement on their credit default swaps from AIG.

Let's look at what I am talking about. During the 2008 meltdown, President Bush had, as chief of staff, Joshua Bolten, who was a former executive from Goldman Sachs. Bush's brother, George H.W. IV was a senior VP and partner at Goldman Sachs, and his Secretary of Treasury was a former CEO from Goldman Sachs. But the Bush administration was no different than the Clinton administration where the Secretary of Treasury Robert Rubin was also a former CEO from Goldman Sachs. And presently, in the Obama administration, there are thirteen executives from Goldman Sachs.

Here is just one case where one firm has an enormous influence on how our government will react to a financial crisis or will react to legislation that is proposed by Congress to regulate their industry. They act as a steel curtain to prevent substantial reform in their industry.

The revelations that Geithner was instrumental in stopping *American International Group (AIG)* from reporting complete and accurate information and, in fact, withholding details from the public about the bailed-out insurer's (AIG) payments to banks during the depths of the financial crisis is not only egregious but was unlawful.

Surely withholding, with intent, information to taxpayers could be a criminal offense. His predecessor to the office of Chairman of the Federal Reserve Bank of New York, Mr. Stephen Friedman, had to leave this office shortly after being appointed because he was trading his Goldman Sachs stock that he had obtained while he was a board member of Goldman Sachs in previous employment. So why would the Federal Reserve Chairman Ben Bernanke appoint a man who obviously had a conflict of interest? Thank goodness the *Wall Street Journal* ferreted out this information and presented an exposé that forced Mr. Friedman to resign. But without this transparency, the public would never had known, and the New York Federal Reserve would have another self-serving head carrying out the will of Wall Street brokerage firms, including Goldman Sachs.

Another thing that the public is not aware of is that these folks from Wall Street do not have to pay capital gains tax when they come into the administration. Because they are divesting themselves of their assets to avoid (the appearance of) conflict of interest, they are relieved of paying taxes on their stock gains or any other gains they have accumulated. Why is this? Paulson admitted as much in open public hearings when I questioned him. It would seem as though going to work for the each administration is an estate-planning technique for the rich to avoid taxes.

Another egregious example of conflict of interest is the former Secretary of Treasury under President Clinton, Robert Rubin. He is on talk shows now and in *Newsweek* special edition issues discussing what went wrong with the economy and how to get it back on track.[52] How it is that this individual has not suffocated under the weight of his own hypocrisy is a mystery to me.

He lobbied for Citigroup as a board member and senior counselor for them to be bailed out by both Paulson and Geithner. He was another former CEO of Goldman Sachs. He has had stints at the World Bank and works as an unofficial economic advisor to President Obama. He has not apologized for his key role played as Treasury Secretary in getting the economy off track in the first place.

Mr. Rubin was ten years at Citibank, and during that time, Citibank had to be saved by the American taxpayers. Yet no word from him on this bungling while Secretary of Treasury, nor regarding his role in eliminating the Glass-Steagall Act, which separated brokerage houses from banks.

> But that's how our system "works" these days: Someone like Rubin is able to wreak destruction, collect an ungodly profit, then go along his merry way, pontificating about how "markets have an inherent and inevitable tendency—probably rooted in human nature—to go to excess both on the upside and the downside."[53]

He was, from the very beginning, against the regulation of derivatives, which was a key factor in the meltdown. The real question is, how long will the public put up with this pontification *and farcical* financial gimmicky?

During the depression, under FDR, the government worked out a plan to help home mortgage borrowers who were in default. No such plan was worked out for folks in this crisis, however. Only lip service. Both the Bush and Obama administrations pushed the banks to do it through a voluntary basis, but not providing money to shore up these loans by giving banks incentives to do this. Instead Secretary Paulson pulled a bait-and-switch maneuver with his TARP program of $750 billion. Ten days after Congress approved the TARP bailout, Paulson decided not to purchase the toxic loan as he had strenuously (and disingenuously) argued, but rather he started bailing out the top fifteen banks that need capital to survive. They were too big to fail. He also bailed out AIG, which in turn bailed out Goldman Sachs and other brokerage firms, including foreign banks in France and China, with taxpayer's money. He changed his tune and had no remorse about doing so. (The reader can see *my aggressive questioning* of Mr. Paulson at: (https://www.youtube.com/watch?v=-hhPvas-Q8Y).

Where was the help for Main Street? Where was the idea of "moral hazard" in this equation, and what about the ubiquitous term from economist Joseph Schumpeter about "creative destruction"? Are we not to allow these folks to fail who made bad economic decisions so that they will not continue their *bad behavior?* If we do not, then we will get more of the same. More meltdowns.

What is really happening is that capitalism is being thwarted, and socialism is succeeding into every fabric of our lives. Ironically, Schumpeter predicted this as well as Marx. Both individuals said capitalism would not survive. Alan Greenspan and George Will are often quoted on the value and purpose of "creative destruction." But it does not occur with the big corporations. Are we going to allow this to occur forever? Fannie Mae, Freddie Mac? Why not privatize them immediately? What we have is creeping socialism, and we have allowed our government to be infiltrated by a shadow government of lobbyists currying favors for their former employer: whether it is Goldman Sachs or pharmaceutical companies, or you name it. We do indeed need a Tea Party or third party to change this mess.

We need to fight back. That is why I sponsored a bill entitled the Financial Industry Reform Act that will not allow private-sector employees to come into any administration until a year after they have divested their stock holdings in companies they have worked for. In other words, no one can work in government until one year after they sold their stock or capital investments that would create a conflict of interest. And they will have to pay all capital gains on these investments and will not gain tax-free status upon going into government service. Also, I would like to extend, for two years (from one year now), the ability of members of Congress to become lobbyists on the Hill after serving in Congress. This bill went nowhere.

We also need to reinstate the Glass-Steagall Act that separates the brokerage houses from banks. As it is now, Goldman Sachs and others can make huge leverage investments sometimes at 30:1 and have the full faith of the United States Government through FDIC indirectly backing their investments in the event of failure. They use the FDIC to pump their bonds and money funds and even go so far as to get loans from the Federal Reserve at zero percent. They then, in turn, loan out money for the purchase of financial securities for their clients at the expense of taxpayers. Isn't this contrary to the intention of the bankers who set up the Federal Reserve? Obviously the Federal Reserve should, itself, be audited and not allowed to loan to these brokerage houses, nor allowed to loan to foreign banks as occurred in the financial meltdown.

Chapter 21
Socialism Around the World

I have had the opportunity to visit *many countries*, and one of the first things I always ask myself when I get there is: Can I drink the water out of the hotel faucet, and if not, why not? I am not of a strong physical constitution, so I dare not try unless it is a western European country or Canada or the United States. I also ask as a second question: Is this country operating under a free economic system, or to what extent is it socialized?

If it is, why? If not, why not?

Generally, most of the countries I have visited are socialized. Not that the government controls all the businesses, but the government operates in a deficit mode, inflates the currency and has a huge entitlements program for its citizens. It is interesting to note that socialism is the most popular idea of any kind, "surpassing even the great religions."[54] In fact, no religion has ever spread so rapidly so far and so fast. Islam conquered an empire that, at its height, embraced twenty percent of mankind. It took 300 years before Christianity could speak for ten percent of the world's people, and after two millennia, it can claim the adherence of about one third of the human race.

By comparison, within 150 years after the followers of Robert Owen from England—who started communes in the United States and coined the term "socialism" in the late 1820s—roughly sixty percent of the Earth's population found itself living under socialist rule of one kind or another.[55]

While it finally collapsed in Russia, it is still popular and accounts for most of the governments of the world today. It is taken up with ardor in China, Africa, India and most of Latin America and also in the Middle East. So today we have governments of social democrats or Third World socialist regimes governing most of the world.

There are two things I wish to say about this spread of socialism. One is that, if the government is overly controlling, then the people ultimately suffer because of the dismal economic performance of the economy. Socialism makes things worse. And the second thing is that the socialist regimes lead to insolvency. Because you have slackers, it becomes a "paradise for parasites."[56] People would expect the government to take care of them, and the government does till eventually there is an economic crisis and people leave the country. As one person said who was a member of the kibbutz in Hamadia: "People like me who started as socialists concluded that you can work hard and get nothing while others don't work hard. It is so unfair."[57]

Today, it is all but universally acknowledged that the wealth that sustains the public sector is created in the private sector. This means that any attempt to expand the public sector beyond a certain point will backfire. If the private sector is squeezed too hard, government revenues will dry up. Thus, it is within the context of predominantly capitalist economics that democratic societies will continue to debate about and experiment with relatively minor variations in taxes and social services.[58]

In America, the possibility of economic opportunity and the self-confidence of an open society make the working man feel he could get rich *someday*. This feeling sustains him, and he does not look for the government to solve his problems. But that is changing in America with continued economic crises, government bailouts, and more newly created federal programs for the displaced.

Unless we educated our citizens and create a better economy which is based upon self-reliance of its people, we are doomed. The government must accept the moral hazard for those companies who exploited the economic situation and got overextended because of incompetence and greed. We must allow them to go bankrupt. If we do not, we will forever move this country towards Western European socialism and a bigger and bigger government, which is totally against what America was based upon. Liberty is freedom with bridled morality. Without this morality, America will become one big failed system controlled by bureaucrats. They become the elite, and the citizens become the slaves.

So from my experience, the more the country moves towards socialism, the less chance that the water is drinkable from the faucet, and the more I have to rely on bottled water.

Chapter 22
Breeding Contempt for the Law

....

"TO IMPEACH OR NOT TO IMPEACH?"
BY REP. CLIFF STEARNS
SPEAKING OUT, *GAINESVILLE SUN*,
THURSDAY, DECEMBER 17, 1998

There can be no free society without law administered through an independent judiciary. If one man can be allowed to determine for himself what is law, every man can. That means first chaos, then tyranny. Legal process is an essential part of the democratic process. [59]

—Supreme Court Justice Felix Frankfurter (1947)

Without the rule of law, the law of the jungle would prevail—the strong would prey upon the weak, the many would oppress the few, and justice would perish. The judicial system stands in the breach, imposing a rational means for protecting our society. This occurs in many thousands of courtrooms throughout America, where punishments are handed down and rights protected.

So much of the judicial process hinges on an individual raising their right hand and swearing to tell the truth. Although a simple act, physically, its impact is extremely profound. Sworn testimony in a court literally can mean the difference between life and death.

Without truth, justice could not exist. That is why we as a society place a premium on the truth. As a result perjury, subornation of perjury, obstruction of justice, and witness tampering are serious criminal offenses.

No matter how powerful, or how popular, or how busy a person may be, no one can be allowed to introduce the poison of perjury into legal proceedings and escape the consequences.

As a member of the House of Representatives, I was presented with extensive and compelling evidence that President Clinton committed perjury, suborned perjury, obstructed justice, and tampered with witnesses.

That is why I voted for all the articles of impeachment.

Earlier that year, President Clinton's attorney general, Janet Reno, broadened Judge Kenneth Starr's investigation to include the Lewinsky matter. A three-judge panel approved this action. As required under the Independent Counsel Act, in September Judge Starr sent a referral outlining the potential impeachable offenses he had found. It contained eleven specific charges of wrongdoing by President Clinton in four areas (perjury, obstruction of justice, witness tampering, and abuse of constitutional authority).

Of these, I believe perjury is the most serious because it is a direct assault on the rule of law. The evidence indicates that the President lied under oath in two instances, during a civil deposition and before a federal grand jury. Are we now to look the other way when a President who is sworn to uphold the law apparently committed a felony? Some of my colleagues may think so, but our duty demands otherwise.

Those opposed to impeachment make many spurious claims, including the statement that perjury is rarely prosecuted. As of October 1998, 115 people were serving time in federal prisons for lying under oath in legal proceedings. The special anguish of 115 families on visiting day illuminates the lie behind this assertion. Equally vacuous is the claim by many that the President did not commit perjury—gave false testimony, yes, but not perjury. The twists they apply to logic are for obfuscation, not for clarification.

For months, the President's advocates have failed to contest the facts of the case. They attacked the Independent Counsel and his staff, but they never offered to contradict the merits of the case built by Judge Starr. They shrieked about partisanship, yet offered no new evidence to clear the President. Shakespeare recognized this desperation as "sound and fury signifying nothing."

The salient point is whether or not Bill Clinton lied under oath. We know what Judge Starr reported, but what does President Clinton's own White House Counsel say on this matter? During testimony before the House Judiciary Committee, Charles Ruff conceded, "Reasonable people ... could determine that he crossed over that line and that what for him was truthful ... was in fact false." That same day, former Massachusetts Governor William Weld, another witness tapped by the White House to plead their case, admitted that he "assumed perjury" had been committed by Mr. Clinton.

The last line of defense for Mr. Clinton's supporters is arguing that perjury is not an impeachable offense. The Constitution establishes impeachment for "Treason, Bribery, or other High Crimes and Misdemeanors." Providing false testimony before a federal grand jury surely must qualify for a high crime or misdemeanor. The third edition of Black's Law Dictionary, a commonly used legal resource, states:

"High crimes and misdemeanors are such immoral and unlawful acts as are nearly (sic) allied and equal in guilt to felony, yet, owing to some technical circumstance, do not fall within the definition of 'felony.'"

Perjury is punishable for up to five years in a federal prison and a fine of up to $30,000. The same judicial system provides lesser penalties for violent crimes, clearly underscoring the importance placed on preserving truthful testimony.

The alternative White House loyalists propose would allow the President to finish his term before he would have to answer for his alleged crimes. They appear undisturbed that a possible serial felon would continue to wield power from the Oval Office. This is a situation which cries out for impeachment.

It is reported that the President's lawyers are operating under the assumption that Judge Starr submitted a sealed indictment of the President to U.S. District Judge Norma Johnson. Such an indictment would become active once Mr. Clinton leaves office. The President is keenly aware of the possibility that shortly after noon on January 20, 2001, federal law enforcement agents could place him under arrest and take him before a U.S. District Judge for arraignment. This means that even if the impeachment vote fails, the President will still be in legal jeopardy. This must weigh heavily on his mind and affect his ability to do this difficult job. Again, this is a situation that demands impeachment.

Impeachment does not decide the guilt or innocence of the President. By exercising our impeachment power, the House is merely acting as a grand jury would, looking for probable cause and then referring the matter for trial, in this case to the Senate. Our duty in the House is to decide if the available evidence indicates that the Senate should consider removing the President from office. I believe that there is sufficient evidence to approve articles of impeachment and to send this process to that next step.

Our society is in trouble. A dark cynicism has taken hold across the land, shaking our faith in our ability to do what is right. The rule of law is one of the few remaining counterweights that keep us from falling into the abyss of anarchy. By placing himself above the rule of law, President Clinton is breeding contempt for the law that serves us all. And should we abandon the law, we will turn our backs on justice and forfeit our right to call ourselves civilized.

——

Statement by Rep. Cliff Stearns
During Impeachment Debate (Contempt for the Law)
HOUSE FLOOR December 18, 1998

Mr. Speaker:

It is with great sorrow that I take the floor to express my support for approving these articles of impeachment of the President. Sorrow because we have come to this point in our fair and wonderful country where we have to debate these articles.

We are all bound together as citizens of this great nation, and as citizens, we are all answerable to the same laws, including President Clinton. The President is more than America's chief law enforcement officer. He is also the trustee of the nation's conscience.

It is a fact the sworn testimony can literally mean the difference between life and death. Should we betray the rule of law by sweeping the President's activities under the rug?

If the opponents of impeachment wanted to avoid this process, they should have mounted a vigorous defense of the President by refuting the facts of the Starr referral. The Minority Leader, the gentleman form Missouri (Mr. Gephardt) mentioned trust, fairness, forgiveness, and values, but I did not hear him mention the word truth. Those against impeachment have not contradicted one word of testimony contained in the 60,000 pages of evidence, not one scintilla.

Those against impeachment should make their case based upon the facts. Are we to conclude that the actions outlined in these four articles of impeachment are permissible behavior for the Chief Executive? Any military officer, from general to private, would be court martialed. Any private citizen would risk prosecution. Any church leader, CEO of a Fortune 500 company, high school faculty member, or community leader would not face censure, they would be fired for similar conduct.

Impeachment does not determine the guilt or innocence of the President. We do not need to be convinced beyond a reasonable doubt to move forward. Our duty in the House is to decide if the available evidence indicates that the Senate should consider removing the President from office.

I believe that there is sufficient evidence to approve these articles of impeachment and to send this process to that next step. Through this vote we shall announce how we stand on the Constitution and the rule of law. Are these outdated concepts to be ignored when convenient, or are they the guiding principles of our American civilization?

Chapter 23
Does Divine Law Exist?

Didn't every country get developed out of murder, deception, infanticide, cannibalism, adultery, regicide, murder and other crimes? No matter where you go in history, you see crimes of vengeance. Aren't all cities founded on such crimes? Notwithstanding the above, there is a divine rule of law where the cycle of vengeance can be overcome.

Yes, civilization is indeed founded upon on acts of original criminality. If it is not solved, then the country oscillates between anarchy and tyranny.[60] It is not just the Bible that provides these truths. Other cultures also describe these divine laws.

Twenty-five hundred years ago in the *Oresteia*—a trilogy of Greek plays by Aeschylus—the question of divine law was presented. If the powerful win every time by sheer power, then humanity goes to the wall.

In this play, Aeschylus shows that personal vengeance must give way to the rule of law, individual revenge to public law and political institutions. Impartial courts must prevail. While good institutions are certainly an advance on private law and private justice, their success depends on their being run by men of good will, which is not often the case.

Likewise in *Antigone*, by Sophocles, we can see the divine law set against the merely human law, and Antigone's stature derives from being in the right. So in this play, human laws are secondary to divine ones, and the government official Creon is making decisions on the basis of political expediency, whereas, Antigone is making her argument based upon conviction in her rectitude. She is working off the divine law, unlike the manmade law of Creon and other rulers.[61]

Both of these plays show that people know instinctively what is right and what should be done, even 2,500 years ago. The sin of man oftentimes prevents him from doing what is correct. Both of these plays show that there is a natural or divine law to take into account with every decision. And the rule of law must take these divine attributes into account.

The fundamental question is, do we have the ability to do what is right? These two plays indicate that we do know *what the right thing to do is*. But depending upon our own morality, this will determine if we will do the right thing. The same is true for our legislators and the President.

So the question of interest is whether you can separate morality from politics. Obviously you should not, but many civilizations did, including ours. Our dealing with the Native American Indian was immoral as well as our continued acceptance of slavery until the passage of the Thirteenth Constitutional Amendment in 1865.

Chapter 24
Limited Government

Unlimited Administration

In the forty-fifth of the *Federalist Papers,* James Madison outlined that the new United States government would create a government of limited powers. He said, "The powers delegated by the proposed Constitution to the federal government are few and defined ... (and) will be exercised principally on external objects, as war, peace, negotiation, and foreign commerce."[62]

What a difference *240-plus* years makes. On October 3, 2008, Congress passed and the President signed the Emergency Economic Stabilization Act, which would allow the Secretary of the Treasury to spend up to $750 billion in such as a fashion as he saw fit to promote and establish market stability. For example, section *101(a) (1)* says, "he (Treasury Secretary) is authorized to purchase ... troubled assets from any financial institution, on such terms and conditions as are determined by the Secretary ..."

Further in this section, if there was any doubt of his authority, in 101(c) it clarifies that "he (Treasury Secretary) is authorized to take such actions as the Secretary deems necessary to carry out the authorities in this Act ..."

So it is up to one man to protect the taxpayers and right side the economy. Was he going to help families keep their homes? No, he bailed out the fifteen largest banks and allowed the brokerage firms to become banks to cover their risks backed up by the FDIC. Was he worried about constraints on his discretion? How was Congress to supervise this enormous expenditure?

But the biggest problem, as pointed out by Gary S. Lawson, Professor of Law at the Boston University School of Law—and a founding member of the Federalist Society—was that there were no constitutional objections to the provisions in the bill, a bill which allowed one man to have this much power. Can Congress delegate this power to one man? Not according to our Constitution of limited government. The Secretary was given sweeping and effectively limitless discretion. But why? Because one man scared the entire federal government and then, after a bait-and-switch tactic, bailed out the "too big to fail" banks instead of buying up the toxic loans as he originally intended, and he convinced Congress that it was necessary. As Mr. Lawson has indicated, there are no such provisions in the Constitution to allow the Secretary to do what he did. And Congress operated outside of the Constitution in approving this act. I voted against this Act.

Again, to quote Mr. Lawson in his analysis of this Act:

> "In sum, the Constitution of 1788 sets up a Congress with relatively limited jurisdiction both to regulate and to spend; and a president with law implementing but not lawmaking, powers that cannot be fragmented away and given to uncontrollable subordinates." He goes on to say, "Moreover, while there have been 27 amendments to the Constitution since 1788, none of those amendments alters the structure and allocation of federal powers.... There is no amendment giving Congress power to regulate manufacturing, agriculture, or construction and no amendment saying that executive or judicial actors can also exercise non-executive or non-judicial functions."
>
> In other words, the world has changed a great deal since 1788, but with respect to the basic structure and powers of the federal government, the Constitution of 1788 has not.[63]

Simply put, our government and Congress went wild. We cannot give up the fight to roll back this Administrative State.

Otherwise, unlimited Big Government will take over, and our country will not be bound by the Constitution but become an Administrative State. We will be like Western Europe but worse.

Everywhere on the globe, socialism has failed, yet with this one act we have further moved America towards government control. When we practice Keynesian economics, we are saying that it is the responsibility of the government to get the economy moving again even if it has to borrow money and assume mounting debt to do so. Rather than get rid of the problem, which caused the economic slide, Keynesian policies promoted the idea that government has all the answers. Today John Maynard Keynes rules the world from the grave. He advocated policies for reducing unemployment and expanding the economy that today finds us with huge deficits and government activism.[64] This amount of colossal debt gives away our sovereignty and moves us, ever closer, to the establishment of a one-world government and economic system. This bailout moved us in that direction.

I believe we could have solved the problem by going directly to the source of the entire housing bubble. Instead of bailing out the brokerage firms, help the homeowners with temporary change in lower interest rates, longer amortization schedules, and perhaps interest-only mortgages. Allow the market to work in some cases and in others cases handle it like we did in the Savings and Loan in crisis. We set up Resolution Trust Corporation and collected all of these assets and sold them back to the private sector. Yes the government did take some losses, but we were not bailing out S&L financial institutions. They failed and we moved on. Let the states handle the insurance claims from AIG and make the brokerage houses get reimbursed ten cents on the dollar rather *than* a hundred percent as the Inspector General of the Treasury indicated should have been done. Here are some questions that need to be answered by the Financial Market Commission set up by Congress to investigate what happened:

If Goldman Sachs was really hedged as the New York Federal Reserve Chairman Stephen Friedman claimed, why did taxpayers pay the investment banks a hundred cents on the dollar?[65]

Did Goldman Sachs and others drive down the value of securities to collect cash, then demand to be made whole and, at the same time, buy credit-default-swap insurance on AIG, while they were helping to sink AIG?[66] Is that legal and ethical?

Why did the New York Fed buy paper at 50 cents on the dollar and pay banks 100 cents, when they had no idea what the intrinsic value of those securities was at the time?[67]

Who really leaned on the New York Fed to not disclose who got our taxpayer money?[68]

Before bailing out any brokerage firm, why didn't the government look at the trade blotters of these trading desks to determine what trading strategy those traders employed during this period and later when making record profits?[69]

Why has the United States government allowed a cabal of financial interests to hijack America?[70]

A fundamental question for Congress and the American people is this: Is Wall Street, through its risky and exotic financial devices, affecting our economy, and what should we do about it?

And lastly, if the taxpayers are going to bail out a corporation or loan them money, they should look at their books and determine if there is fraud first and then restrict them, much like a judge would do if they were in bankruptcy. The executives should not be allowed to give themselves big bonuses and stock options while they are practically insolvent with taxpayer's money. For example, when the government went in to take over AIG, they should have gone to the source of the problem, which was the wholly owned, London-based financial-products subsidiary of AIG that had written hundreds of billions of dollars of credit-default-swaps contracts on exotic collateralized debt obligations (CDOs).[71]

Since AIG ran out of cash to make the collateral calls, should these people be rewarded? Put those people in jail and settle five to ten cents on the dollar, including with the foreign banks.[72] But the biggest recipient of the cash siphoned from taxpayers was Goldman Sachs.

Eliminate the conflict of interest within every Administration by preventing executives from one firm to continually dominate. Make them sell all their assets before they come into the administration one year in advance and do not allow them to escape capital gains taxes as they now do when they come into each administration. Audit the Federal Reserve every year and publish their results. Immediately break up corporations that are too big to fail and force banks and brokerage houses to keep a higher ratio of liquid capital on their books. Reinstate the Glass-Steagall Act, which separates banks and brokerage institutions—the latter purchase financial commodities sometimes at 30:1 leverage. Taxpayers should not have to insure this kind of risk. Get full transparency between the Treasury, Federal Reserve and each local Federal Reserve, especially the New York Federal Reserve.

All of us hope and pray that the newly instituted "Financial Crisis Inquiry Commission" (FCIC) that has the authority to investigate the causes, domestic and global, of the financial and economic *meltdown/crisis* will succeed. All hope that they will make recommendations on how to avoid future meltdowns. I doubt if they will be successful. *(They were not successful!) They needed* a bulldog attorney who knows more about Wall Street than Wall Street. One man could make a difference.

Postscript: The FCIC failed to identify any culpable executives nor did they even adequately explain how the great recession started, who was to blame, and how we can prevent it again. The best article on this is the interview by Jessica Pressler (in *New York* magazine, December 28, 2015)[73] with Michael Burry, the real-life market genius portrayed in the movie *The Big Short*. His fear is that there is another financial crisis looming, and the Dodd-Frank legislation that passed Congress will not fix the problems.

Chapter 25
Travel and Congressional Delegation Trips

Jimmy Miller's World Travel Club

In the entire world, there is probably nothing better than travel. But traveling as a Congressman is perhaps the best perk of the job. When you go on a congressional trip you have your own plane, and generally it is a Boeing 727 fully equipment and updated. Plus you are escorted by the military, generally the Marines or the Air Force. Your status as a member of Congress, whether Senator or Congressman, means that your diplomatic status is higher than that of a four-star general. So everywhere that you go, you are treated with the respect accorded a head of state. You can meet the president of the country as well as the leaders of the various political parties. Plus you have at your disposal the American Embassy and State Department. So much can be scheduled in two days that, generally, with the help of all these folks, you are able to meet and see the environs and all the important leaders without any wasted time.

In the twenty-four years I have been in Congress, I have been *to many countries* and countless cities. On many of these trips, you can bring your spouse along. It is especially nice to enjoy these special trips with *your wife*. So often you meet second and third wives on these trips, especially with senior members. The question is often asked, "How do you get invited on these *trips?*" *Generally* you have to work within your committee assignments and through the approval of your chairman or through friends of yours who tip you off to the eligibility of certain trips. The Transportation Committee and the International Affairs Committee go on the most trips, with the Appropriations Committee not far behind.

I would make a strong argument that these trips are very useful job-wise. The press and the voters will not agree, but as a member of Congress you have to vote on things that affect the entire world, and you also must see and know what the real world is like outside DC and your congressional district. I do not doubt it is costly—and oft times abused. The press sometimes follows these trips and sets up cameras close to the events to see who attends or to show the lifestyle of the trip. But meeting the heads of state of these various countries, and also the people who live in these countries, goes a long way towards understanding how America should act.

It is quite tiring to go to three or four countries in ten days without very much sleep. Between the time changes and the warm rooms, sonorous presentations—countless PowerPoint slides in darkened rooms—you come home exhausted and aged. Nevertheless, after a couple of days of rest, you are always glad you went. The memory of the last trip plants the seeds of the next.

Without the aid of the military and the coordination by our embassies, one could never hope to accomplish so much in so little time. There is another aspect about this traveling that is very rewarding, and that is meeting, socializing and befriending fellow members, especially from the other party. On these trips, you develop lasting friendships and get to know members you would never know except on these trips. It comes in handy when you are trying to broker legislation and develop support for your position.

Another aspect of these trips, which is special, is that every place you arrive, the military sets up a delegation room at the hotel where you have access to computers, printers, news clips and newspapers, snacks and telephones. Most delegates have *their BlackBerries and iPhones* [or various smart devices today] but oftentimes it is nice to call home to your staff on a secured line. The military picks up your bags at every stop and delivers them to your room without fail; this helps with the processing time. On every trip there is a military doctor who helps spouses and members for sickness, which invariably occurs, especially when we go *to Asia* or South America.

Members generally purchase artifacts, rugs and artwork to bring home. This is perhaps the most embarrassing aspect of the sojourns. Since you rarely pay sales tax, and you are getting discounts through the embassy, people buy more than they should or need and load up the plane to such a degree that it is embarrassing. When the plane is finally unloaded at Andrews AFB, the luggage taken off the plane is enormous and superfluous. Of course you know that you don't need half the stuff you buy, but at the time, the creeping thought is, *I might never be here again*. In India, members bought so many rugs and presents that I took a photo of it just so I could see it later for my own eyes. Members making a good salary, which they all are, of course, act as if they are stocking their own museum!

One of the best ways to travel is with the Transportation Committee. On their staff is a former non-commission officer (NCO) by the name of Jimmy Miller. Once an Air Force warrant officer, Jimmy Miller was well traveled before he retired from the *Air Force* and had a lot of experience in worldwide travel. He is a wonderful ingenious fellow who can find anything for you and knows how to make things work, both mechanically and process-wise. He is just a delight and fun to travel with. He has been everywhere, and when you go with him, you enjoy the best trips.

Several members have traveled numerous times with him and have coined a name for the privilege: The Jimmy Miller Worldwide Travel Club. To be a member you have to be sworn in and take an oath. Jimmy Miller will administer the oath on the plane once it has reached cruising altitude. The oath goes like this:

"I (state your name) do earnestly swear that I will abide by the rules and regulations of The Jimmy Miller Worldwide Travel Club to the best of my abilities and will agree not to ask a lot of questions, especially when the lights are low and the day is late. And you take this solemn oath to protect and owe allegiance to its members. Do you solemnly swear? I do. Congratulations."

The simple camaraderie and good fellowship that goes along with this ceremony does much to make the group harmonious and courteous to each other. When you lose sleep and compress so much into one day, oftentimes members and their spouses get irritable and sick. It takes patience sometime to accommodate others when they are disagreeable and impolite.

As co-chairman of the Air Force Congressional Caucus, I led trips to Iraq, Afghanistan and Kuwait. When all is said and done, travel is special, but going as a member of Congress is particularly special. No matter how much money you have, you cannot duplicate the mission and sense of purpose and degree of attention that you obtain when traveling as an ambassador for the United States of America.

Conclusion

After twenty-four years, I have seen it all, the fake budgets and the competing fake budgets. No President in any administration in which I served offered a real balanced budget, which included Social Security, Medicare and Medicaid.

What should be done?

I think, again, we should go back to something Thomas Jefferson wrote in a letter to John Taylor in November of 1798:

> I wish it were possible to obtain a single amendment to our Constitution. I would be willing to depend on that alone for the reduction of the administration of our government to the genuine principles of its Constitution. I mean an additional article, taking from the federal government the power of borrowing.[74]

We have had a War in Iraq, and President Bush did not put the war effort on budget, but instead just offered supplemental spending amendments to cover the cost. This could only be financed by borrowing because the taxpayers would not make the sacrifice to pay for the war, so the cost had to be hidden. There were no checks and balances here because the Republicans, including myself, voted for this spending.

But debt will destroy our country. Going back to Jefferson, he reiterated several times that one generation cannot—either morally or in fact—bind another. He stipulated, "No generation can contract debts greater than may be paid during the course of its own existence."[75] And further, he said that "the earth belongs in usufruct [trust] to the living ... the dead have neither powers nor rights over it."[76] If one generation can charge another for its debts, "then the earth would belong to the dead and not to the living generation."[77] Jefferson continued, "The conclusion then, is, that neither the representatives of a nation, nor the whole nation itself assembled, can validly engage debts beyond what they may pay in their own time."[78] Madison did not agree and used the example of a large bridge, but Jefferson argued that there could be no exception because the power to borrow was too dangerous to allow exceptions—any exceptions would expand to destroy the amendment.

I would strongly argue that the Jefferson amendment is necessary and, with the exception of total war, must be paid for by the present generation, and even with war, the present generation must make sacrifices to pay for the effort.[79]

Another lesson is to limit the power of the federal government through federalism, which I mentioned earlier. This balance between the states and the federal government is the balance that was required to keep the country safe from plutocracy in all its forms and in all its locations—banks, the military, and governments. The destruction of states' rights and the centralization of power unchecked in the federal government have contributed to what is today called the Imperial Presidency. It was never intended that the President could force through his own legislation without Congress's intervening and reaction. Today, Congress pretty much follows the President's desires almost as leadership worship, except when his party is not in power. Isn't his job to mainly to be sure that the law of the land is enforced and enact a legal foreign policy—and nothing else?

The framers of our Constitution realized how important the rule of law was and is still and knew how the English monarchs used the courts to serve their own purposes. They also understood there could be no order without law, no law without morality, and no morality without religion. They were not the kind of secular humanists that are so prevalent in our country today. The President should spend more time in office protecting these laws.[80]

And lastly, I firmly believe we need to sunset many, if not all, of the government programs and carefully evaluate the good ones and consolidate programs to protect the taxpayers from duplication and waste. Even under the Republican revolution, we could not shut down any government programs. In fact, when I had amendments to reduce the budget by one percent across the board, they all failed! I have even tried to reduce some programs that represented *less than* one percent, and again Congress did not have the courage to even make this reduction.

If Congress cannot do this, then a base-closure commission, like we did for the military bases, should be set up to eliminate and reduce obsolete and unnecessary government programs. Without this type of action, our government will continue to grow and the bureaucracy will ultimately be too strong to counteract.

Time and time again, I see votes on the House floor that have wonderful names to them, such as the Habitat for Pelicans, the Protection of Wildlife Reserves, Save Our Water Restoration Act and so on. These pieces of legislation are brought up under what is called suspension, i.e., without going through regular order, with no ability to amend them. They pass overwhelmingly because members just assume they are good. But they cost money, and when you are operating in a deficit mode, you cannot afford them. But they pass anyway.

What we need in all cases is wisdom—this is not specially directed towards America but to all countries and to individuals. They are seven demonstrations of these wisdoms, which we should remind ourselves.[81]

1. Fear of the Lord

2. Humility

3. Knowledge

4. Right action

5. Wisdom (Experience)

6. Understanding

7. Counsel

These right actions are as important for an individual as for a country. Without these actions, no country will endure.[82]

Is Thomas Jefferson turning in his grave?

In early 1796, our young nation found itself grappling with a huge amount of national debt, the result of financing our American Revolution. Alexander Hamilton controversially proposed that the federal government assume all the debt states incurred during the Revolution.

However, some states, like Thomas Jefferson's Virginia, had already paid off almost half of its debt and rightly felt that its citizens should not be assessed again to bail out those states that were reckless in their financial decisions. Concerned Americans used this issue to lure Thomas Jefferson out of retirement at Monticello to reduce the mounting national debt and steady the country's shaky economy.

Over two hundred years plus later, we find our country facing economic uncertainty with a rapidly rising national debt and a lingering housing and mortgage crisis. The government-sponsored enterprises (GSEs), the Federal National Mortgage Association (Fannie Mae) and the Federal Home Loan Mortgage Corporation (Freddie Mac), which insure half of the nation's mortgages, are suffering billions in losses and may require government bailout. To be precise, Freddie Mac suffered its fourth straight negative quarter in 2006, with a loss of $821 million. To put this in perspective, they lost $475 million in the third quarter in 2005 while its sister and rival, Fannie Mae, lost a staggering $2.3 billion last quarter. These worse-than-expected losses came just weeks after Congress orchestrated a sweeping effort to prop up the companies, the two biggest providers of U.S. residential mortgage funding, by exposing American taxpayers to a vast financial risk.

These two GSEs are supposed to make the American dream come true, but in fact, they are contributing relatively little to the overall quality of the U.S. housing finance system. At the same time, they have created exorbitant risk for everyone around them. *(And they still do today.)*

It used to be argued that simply chartering Freddie and Fannie didn't mean the federal government was on the hook if they collapsed, but almost nobody makes that case and more. The risk is obvious and two-fold: an implicit financial obligation of the federal government and a dagger aimed at the heart of our national economy.

Freddie and Fannie aren't government agencies, but they pretend to be, and everyone expects the government to bail them out if they get into trouble. Even more serious is what people expect of their government when any too-big-to-fail entity is failing.

Fannie and Freddie have incurred over $5.2 trillion in debt by borrowing $1.5 trillion and guaranteeing mortgage-backed securities worth $3.7 trillion. A loss of even a small portion of these obligations would require the federal government to intervene and save them from their own mistakes, dwarfing the losses generated by the savings-and-loan debacle of twenty years ago.

Investors, believing that the government will not permit Fannie or Freddie to fail, still provide funds at rates that are not commensurate with the risk that these companies represent. They do it in part because GSEs enjoy special privileges and immunities that ordinary private companies can only dream about. Private companies cannot compete with these behemoths on an even footing.

Not long ago, *Former Federal Reserve Board* Chairman Alan Greenspan told the Senate Banking Committee that "the existence, or even the perception, of government backing undermines the effectiveness of market discipline." And he was right.

Part private and part public, Fannie and Freddie's current ailments demonstrate what happens when profits are privatized and risk is not. With the government's backing, they are able to absorb large obligations and retain profits for themselves while leaving taxpayers on the hook when the debts get too big and/or the profits dry up.

Several years ago, I became concerned with the financial picture of both Fannie and Freddie. As a member of the Oversight Subcommittee of the House Energy and Commerce Committee, I participated in the Enron hearings and learned of the fraud and abuses perpetrated through accounting procedures.

I learned that Freddie Mac had famously "misapplied" the Financial Accounting Standard Board's (FASB) standards for derivatives and hedging in its financial statement. A 2003 investigation by the Department of Justice and the U.S. Securities and Exchange Commission revealed a staggering $4.5 billion in accounting errors. Freddie Mac subsequently admitted to distorting its reported earnings between 2000 and 2003, resulting in millions in shareholder lawsuit settlements.

In 2003, as the Chairman of the Subcommittee on Commerce, Trade, and Consumer Protection of the Energy and Commerce Committee, I held hearings on FASB accounting standards, including a hearing in September on the implications of Freddie Mac's fraudulent accounting practices. I planned on holding additional hearings on Freddie Mac's restatement and developing legislation on accounting standards until jurisdiction over FASB was suddenly stripped away from my subcommittee and transferred to the Financial Services Committee—seemingly the result of an intensive lobbying effort on Freddie's part.

The current view in Congress is that if legislation is adopted granting greater regulatory authority to some entity, whether a part of the Treasury or an independent commission, the risk these two companies represent will be significantly reduced.

This might be true if Fannie and Freddie were common companies, but they are not. For starters, they are enormous and, remember, the two own or guarantee *more than half of all* U.S. mortgages. So it should come as no surprise that Fannie and Freddie are among the most politically powerful special interests in Washington, and they're well supported by nearly everyone whose success is linked to housing—those who build houses, who sell them, who make loans, and who underwrite the securities that back those loans.

You might even have the misimpression from their extensive advertising that Fannie and Freddie are in business to house the poor. In fact, they are in business to make money for their shareholders, paying $4 billion in dividends to their shareholders last year, while leaving taxpayers liable for potentially billions in losses.

Only new leadership, a reduction in the size of their gargantuan loan portfolios, and true assumption of risk by their shareholders will get the attention of these dinosaurs.

I can't help but wonder what Thomas Jefferson would think about the current state of our debt-burdened economy and the way the government has allowed GSEs such as Fannie and Freddie to spiral out of control and jeopardize hardworking American taxpayers.

Surely he would purport freeing our economy from the grip of this avoidable financial instability. After all, it was Jefferson who said, "[the] principle of spending money to be paid by posterity, under the name of funding, is but swindling futurity on a large scale."[83]

Thus it seems that the only viable solution left is to put Fannie Mae and Freddie Mac on par with everybody else by removing their hands from the taxpayers' purse. Once everyone understands that Fannie and Freddie have to stand on their own, the invisible hand of market discipline will guide Fannie and Freddie into success, and America will be dramatically more resilient to the economic stresses that bedevil us now and in the future.

In Praise of Folly
The Solyndra Investigation

In Praise of Folly was written by Erasmus to reflect his love of humor and satire, but at the same time, it gives great insight into the political times of his life, which were characterized by intense strife among intellectuals and the populous. We are in a similar situation today.

With spiraling debt in this country, Congress and the Executive Branch are not reducing spending in this country, and our country is headed in the wrong direction, which is why the voters don't trust *Congress* or the President. There is so much waste in Congress and little is being done to stop it. There is no better example of this self-deception and abuse of the Executive Branch and the lack of will of Congressional oversight than the Solyndra investigation.

As Chairman of the Oversight & Investigation Subcommittee of Energy and Commerce, I led a team of eleven lawyers plus administrative staff with subpoena power. It was the same committee that Congressman John Dingell (D-Michigan), the Dean of the House of Representative, chaired for decades—and with it he wielded immense power. But we were stymied. This lack of proactive jurisdiction by Congress contributed to Rep. John Boehner's demise as the Speaker of the House of Representatives.

Lack of follow-through with the procedural requirements checking the power of the President and the Executive Branch would occur almost every month during his tenure as Speaker. A case in point was my Congressional investigation and oversight of the Executive

Branch through the loss of $536 million of taxpayer's money provided with a loan guarantee to Solyndra by the Department of Energy. The company lied about its solvency, and the Administration continued to prop it up and cover up its activities even though there were emails within the Department of Energy that the company was not solvent. The Executive Branch wanted to make Solyndra a showcase of solar technology and alternative energy capabilities and innovation.

Solyndra was a manufacturer of cylindrical panels of copper indium gallium selenide (CIGS), thin film solar cells based in Fremont, California. Although the company was once touted for its unusual technology, plummeting silicon prices led to the company's inability to compete with conventional solar panels made of crystalline silicon.[84] The *company* filed for bankruptcy on September 1, 2011.

Solyndra received a $536 million U.S. Energy Department loan guarantee, the first recipient of a loan guarantee under President Barack Obama's economic stimulus program, the American Recovery and Reinvestment Act of 2009. Additionally, Solyndra received a $25.1 million tax break from California's Alternative Energy and Advanced Transportation Financing Authority.[85] Shortly after this, the FBI raided Solyndra for fraud and started its own investigation.

Ultimately it went bankrupt and contributors to President Obama's campaign gained access to its bankruptcy assets at the expense of taxpayers who were forced, illegally, to be subordinated to these campaign contributors.[86] These contributors used this bankruptcy loss for their own write-offs with their existing corporations and to gain the assets at pennies on the dollar. We had Congressional oversight authority, but it was not used properly, and our many subpoenas to the White House were never fully complied with even after eight months. On August 31, 2011, Solyndra announced it was filing for Chapter 11 bankruptcy protection, laying off 1,100 employees and shutting down all operations and manufacturing.[87]

My request to issue a contempt of Congress citation on the White House and the Department of Energy was denied by my Republican Leadership, and we were left trying to salvage the investigation as best we could. Our last efforts occurred just after the presidential primaries and could have been a defining example of ineptitude of the Administration.

Following the bankruptcy, the government was expected to recoup $27 million under the Solyndra restructuring plan, but no money was ever recovered.[88]

On August 26, 2015, the federal government reported that "Solyndra, the solar panel manufacturer who took more than $500 million from President Obama's stimulus then went bust, sticking taxpayers for the loss, lied to federal officials to secure the loan, the Energy Department's inspector general said in a report released Wednesday [August 26, 2015]."[89]

This is just one example of the Administration concealing their activities and helping to benefit their contributors. Major investors included George Kaiser Family Foundation, US Venture Partners, CMEA Ventures, Redpoint Ventures, Virgin Green Fund, Madrone Capital Partners, RockPort Capital Partners, Argonaut Private Equity, Masdar and Artis Capital Management.[90]

But no one went to jail, and the Administration never had to answer for the egregious loss of taxpayer's money, i.e., over half a billion dollars. And Secretary of Energy Steven Chu was never fired—though I repeatedly called for his resignation.

The rule of law doesn't seem to apply in politics today.

If the political pundits are wondering today why the American people are so upset and willing to go to outsiders for political solutions, then they only need to follow the Solyndra investigation and see the lack of Congressional oversight on the budget to understand why.

The book *In Praise of Folly* by Erasmus gave insight into the political times of that day. It is my hope that my book will in some small way give new insight into our political times and create change.

THE END

Appendix

–One–

A very interesting new read from the January edition of *Bloomberg Magazine*. Anyone else find it suspicious how many at the meeting were former Goldman executives?

**How Paulson Gave Hedge Funds
Advance Word of Fannie Rescue**

by Richard Teitelbaum
(from Bloomberg Markets) bloomberg.com
November 29, 2011 — 12:46 PM EST

Treasury Secretary Henry Paulson stepped off the elevator into the Third Avenue offices of hedge fund Eton Park Capital Management LP in Manhattan. It was July 21, 2008, and market fears were mounting. Four months earlier, Bear Stearns Cos. had sold itself for just $10 a share to JPMorgan Chase & Co. (JPM).

Now, amid tumbling home prices and near-record foreclosures, attention was focused on a new source of contagion: Fannie Mae (FNMA) and Freddie Mac, which together had more than $5 trillion in mortgage-backed securities and other debt outstanding.

Paulson had been pushing a plan in Congress to open lines of credit to the two struggling firms and to grant authority for the Treasury Department to buy equity in them. Yet he had told reporters on July 13 that the firms must remain shareholder owned and had testified at a Senate hearing two days later that giving the government new power to intervene made actual intervention improbable.

Continue reading...

http://www.bloomberg.com/news/articles/2011-11-29/how-henry-paulson-gave-hedge-funds-advance-word-of-2008-fannie-mae-rescue

NEWS FROM
North Central Florida's Congressman
CLIFF STEARNS
For Immediate Release November 3, 2010

STEARNS REQUESTS INVESTIGATION BY FINANCIAL COMMISSION INTO CHARGES BY FORMER FEDERAL REGULATORS OF CONFLICT OF INTEREST BY FORMER TREASURY SECRETARY PAULSON

BASED UPON NEW EVIDENCE THAT PAULSON FAILED TO ACT WELL BEFORE THE FINANCIAL MELTDOWN

WASHINGTON, NOV. 3, 2010 – Noting statements by former regulators, Rep. Cliff Stearns (R-FL) is urging the Financial Crisis Inquiry Commission (FCIC) to investigate former Treasury Secretary Henry Paulson who the regulators indicated had a clear conflict of interest and deliberately acted in the best interest of his former firm, Goldman Sachs. Said Stearns, "Mr. Paulson's inaction and perhaps intentional failure to perform a required duty during his first 15 months as Secretary reveal his complicity in putting Wall Street before Main Street." Stearns wrote to Phil Angelides, Chairman of the FCIC, outlining how Paulson failed to take action to address the housing bubble because it would have harmed the financial position of Goldman Sachs (a copy of this letter is attached).

In his letter, Stearns included a statement from former thrift regulator William Black who noted that "No one was better positioned...than Mr. Paulson to understand exactly what the implications of his moving against the (housing) bubble would have been for Goldman Sachs, because he knew what the Goldman Sachs positions were." Mr. Black testified before the FCIC on September 21, 2010, adding that Paulson "knew that if he acted the way he should, that would have burst the bubble. Then Goldman Sachs would have been left with a very substantial loss, and that would have been the end of bonuses at Goldman Sachs."

Stearns also cited a statement to Congress by Richard Newsom, former senior thrift examiner and key investigator of the Lincoln Savings and Loan collapse of the 1980s. Newsome said that it was "simply implausible that Paulson couldn't see the relation between delaying strong action by Treasury and the benefit to letting places like Goldman" reduce their risks.

In addition, Stearns points out that Paulson was not fully divested from Goldman Sachs. Explained Stearns, "An article in the Miami Herald reports that while Paulson made the divestments required under government ethic rules, his wife and son remained trustees of the Paulson's Bobolink Foundation, that held more than $100 million in Goldman Sachs stock."

Privatize Fannie and Freddie
By Rep. Cliff Stearns

It is no secret that our country is facing economic uncertainty with a rapidly rising national debt and a lingering housing and mortgage crisis. Just weeks ago our Congress orchestrated a sweeping effort to prop up government-sponsored enterprises (GSEs) Fannie Mae and Freddie Mac, which own or insure half of the nation's mortgages, by exposing American taxpayers to vast financial risk.

Now, the Treasury recently has finalized a plan to officially bail out Fannie and Freddie — a step I hoped our government wouldn't be forced to take.

It used to be argued that simply chartering Freddie and Fannie didn't mean the federal government was on the hook if these mortgage giants collapsed, but now no one can make that case anymore.

The recent and worrisome events occurring in the U.S. housing market have revealed that the federal government bears significant risk in its chartering of Fannie Mae and Freddie Mac. Although these two GSEs are supposed to make the American dream come true, the reality is they are contributing relatively little to the overall quality of the U.S. housing finance system.

At the same time, they have created exorbitant risks for both taxpayers and the entire economic system that cannot be adequately addressed by regulation alone.

Over the years, Fannie and Freddie have been allowed to incur over $5.2 trillion in debt by borrowing $1.5 trillion and guaranteeing mortgage-backed securities worth $3.7 trillion. Unfortunately, since January of this year, Fannie and Freddie's stock value has also declined by 90%.

The collapse of Fannie and Freddie's common share prices, coupled with the current credit, housing, and mortgage crisis and illiquidity of our markets, has clearly demonstrated that the financial and regulatory structures we have been operating with have failed us.

With the hasty passage of the Housing and Economic Recovery Act (H.R. 3221), Congress granted the Treasury a broad new authority to inject capital into the struggling mortgage giants if need be.

To the surprise of few, with a collapse imminent, the Treasury decided it will transfer control of Fannie and Freddie and place it into conservatorship, which is akin to the filing of Chapter 11 bankruptcy. The Treasury will now commence with buying mortgage-backed securities from banks in the open market at the expense of American taxpayers.

Although this move will probably lower interest rates on home loans — by about 1% — this bailout won't stabilize home prices or swiftly curb the rate of foreclosures, which are currently at an all-time high.

Thus, the immediate effects of this Treasury bailout of Fannie and Freddie will serve to benefit international stock exchanges and large central banks in foreign countries. To be specific, one of the biggest immediate beneficiaries of this bailout will be central banks in Asia, such as the People's Bank of China, which has billions of dollars invested in Fannie Mae and Freddie Mac bonds.

Four years ago Federal Reserve Board Chairman Alan Greenspan told the Senate Banking Committee that "the existence, or even the perception, of government backing undermines the effectiveness of market discipline," and he was right.

We must a find an effective way to free our economy from the grip of this avoidable financial instability. In order to do so, Fannie and Freddie must be restructured and set on a path towards gradual privatization, for placing Fannie and Freddie into conservatorship is not a good long-term solution. Privatization is the most viable solution to mitigating the enormous risks posed by these out-of-control GSEs.

To be sure we never find ourselves in this situation again, Fannie and Freddie must be removed entirely from the government's account, be placed in direct competition with other financial institutions, and be subjected to the effective discipline of the U.S. market.

In this way, we can stabilize these important mortgage firms, restore confidence to investors and shareholders, and relieve American taxpayers from the burden of another costly bailout.

The American people deserve better than what these GSEs have to offer. We cannot allow Fannie and Freddie to leave us with a legacy of debt to be shouldered by hardworking Americans, for as Thomas Jefferson once said, "[the] principle of spending money to be paid by posterity, under the name of funding, is but swindling futurity on a large scale."

–Two–

Steven M. Davidoff, writing as The Deal Professor, is a commentator for *DealBook* on the legal aspects of mergers, private equity and corporate governance. A former corporate lawyer at Shearman & Sterling, he is a professor at the University of Connecticut School of Law. His columns are available at The Deal Professor blog.

8 Questions for Henry Paulson

by Steven M Davidoff
dealbook.nytimes.com
July 16, 2009 8:33 am

> Henry M. Paulson Jr., the former Treasury Secretary, is going before the House Committee on Oversight and Government Reform this morning for a hearing with the agenda "Bank of America and Merrill Lynch: How Did a Private Deal Turn Into a Federal Bailout? Part III."

With such a title, I am sure there will be grandstanding aplenty. But for those members of the House looking for material, I thought I would set forth some of the burning and not-so-burning questions (on my mind, at least) about the Bank of America–Merrill Lynch deal. To be fair to Mr. Paulson, his actions, together with the rest of the government, did save the financial system and he deserves credit for that.

Steven M. Davidoff, writing as The Deal Professor, is a commentator for DealBook on the legal aspects of mergers, private equity and corporate governance. A former corporate lawyer at Shearman & Sterling, he is a professor at the University of Connecticut School of Law. His columns are available at The Deal Professor blog.

Yet, their government-by-deal approach has left some wondering about the consistency of their actions and whether they might have exacerbated certain aspects of the crisis. The government's actions in the Bank of America-Merrill Lynch deal reflect these concerns. While some of this may be attributed to the lack of political and legal authority the government had, as well as the time constraints, it still leaves a number of unanswered questions for Mr. Paulson.

Continue reading…

http://dealbook.nytimes.com//2009/07/16/8-questions-for-hank-paulson/

STEARNS SUBMITS ADDITIONAL QUESTIONS FOR FORMER TREASURY SECRETARY PAULSON

STEARNS ENGAGED PAULSON IN A HEATED EXCHANGE AT OVERSIGHT AND GOVERNMENT REFORM COMMITTEE HEARING*

WASHINGTON, JULY 23, 2009 – Although not a member of the Oversight and Government Reform Committee, Rep. Cliff Stearns (R-Sixth) was provided the opportunity to ask questions at a hearing with former Treasury Secretary Henry Paulson who established the Troubled Assets Relief Program (TARP) and engineered the financial sector bailouts. Today, Stearns submitted additional questions for Paulson through the Oversight and Government Reform Committee.

"Neil Barofsky, TARP Special Inspector General, recently stated that that taxpayers could be exposed to a liability of $23.7 trillion in dealing with the financial crisis," said Stearns. "Paulson was the architect of these bailouts and we need to understand how these bailouts were developed and we need to hold those involved accountable for their actions. I have submitted eight questions that were derived from a popular blog site sponsored by the New York Times. These questions are designed to bring transparency to the machinations in creating TARP, the overall approach in dealing with the financial crisis, and the issue of conflicting interests in using taxpayer dollars."

(Questions from Stearns attached)

* Video of hearing -- http://www.youtube.com/repcliffstearns

–Three–
Letter to Chairman Angelides on Paulson Ethic Conflict

CLIFF STEARNS
6TH DISTRICT, FLORIDA

WASHINGTON
2370 RAYBURN HOUSE OFFICE BUILDING
WASHINGTON, DC 20515-0906
(202) 225-5744
FAX: (202) 225-3973
www.house.gov/stearns

AIR FORCE CAUCUS, Co-Chairman
CHRONIC OBSTRUCTIVE PULMONARY
DISEASE CAUCUS, Co-Chairman
CYSTIC FIBROSIS CAUCUS, Co-Chairman
CONGRESSIONAL HORSE
CAUCUS, Co-Chairman

Congress of the United States
House of Representatives
Washington, DC 20515-0906

COMMITTEE ON ENERGY AND COMMERCE
SUBCOMMITTEES:
COMMUNICATIONS, TECHNOLOGY, AND
THE INTERNET
Ranking Republican Member
ENERGY AND ENVIRONMENT
COMMERCE, TRADE, AND
CONSUMER PROTECTION

COMMITTEE ON VETERANS' AFFAIRS
SUBCOMMITTEES:
HEALTH
OVERSIGHT AND INVESTIGATIONS

October 22, 2010

Phil Angelides
Chairman
Financial Crisis Inquiry Commission
1717 Pennsylvania Ave, N.W.
Suite 800
Washington, DC 20006-4614

Dear Chairman Angelides:

As your work at the congressionally created Financial Crisis Inquiry Commission (FCIC) begins to wind down, I write to draw your attention to a troubling matter involving former Treasury Secretary Henry Paulson, who testified before the Commission in May of this year. New evidence demonstrating Mr. Paulson had a clear conflict of interest during his time as Secretary of the Treasury and deliberately acted in the best interest of his former firm, Goldman Sachs, instead of in the interest of the American people, warrants the immediate attention of this Commission.

In a recent front-page article in the Miami Herald, former senior thrift regulator William Black pointed out that "No one was better positioned…than Mr. Paulson to understand exactly what the implications of his moving against the (housing) bubble would have been for Goldman Sachs, because he knew what the Goldman Sachs positions were." Mr. Black, who testified before the FCIC on September 21, 2010, went on to say that Mr. Paulson "knew that if he acted the way he should, that would have burst the bubble. Then Goldman Sachs would have been left with a very substantial loss, and that would have been the end of bonuses at Goldman Sachs." In addition, Richard Newsom, former senior thrift examiner and key investigator of the Lincoln Savings and Loan debacle of the 1980s, wrote to Congress detailing the regulatory lapses that he believes contributed to the financial crisis and has stated that it was "simply implausible that Paulson couldn't see the relation between delaying strong action by Treasury and the benefit to letting places like Goldman" reduce their risks.

Mr. Paulson's inaction and perhaps intentional failure to perform a required duty during his first 15 months as Secretary reveal his complicity in putting Wall Street before Main Street. During that time of government inaction, Goldman Sachs was able to sell off over $30 billion in toxic residential mortgage securities to pension funds, foreign banks and other investors, thus enabling the firm to safely exit a housing market that was on the brink of collapse. Goldman Sachs also managed to make huge profits by betting against the very securities they were selling to unwitting investors. For this, they faced a civil fraud suit and paid a fine of $550 million to the Securities and Exchange Commission (SEC).

As you are aware, during Mr. Paulson's time at Goldman Sachs as its chief executive, the firm immersed itself into the business of purchasing risky subprime mortgages and subsequently repackaging them into securities and selling them off. Later, Goldman turned around and made billions in profits by betting against those same toxic mortgage securities. Under Mr. Paulson, Goldman Sachs took huge positions in a fraud-infested market. In fact, a much-noted 2006 Business Week article hailed Henry Paulson for being "one of the key architects of a more daring Wall Street, where securities firms are taking greater and greater chances in their pursuit of profits."

Upon becoming Treasury Secretary in mid 2006, Mr. Paulson chose not to address the risky mortgage lending practices that were rampant in the subprime market – the very same practices his former firm, Goldman Sachs, was taking advantage of and that Mr. Paulson himself had overseen as chief executive. What was the reason for Mr. Paulson's inaction?

In addition to Mr. Paulson's seemingly deliberate inaction during his first year as Treasury Secretary, the aforementioned Miami Herald article by Greg Gordon reveals that Mr. Paulson was not fully divested from Goldman Sachs. The article reports that despite other divestments Mr. Paulson was forced to make under government ethics rules, Mr. Paulson's wife and his son remained trustees of the Paulsons' Bobolink Foundation, which was backed by over $100 million in Goldman Sachs stock. According to the article, the Paulsons' foundation still had $33.5 million invested in Goldman Sachs funds more than a year and half into Mr. Paulson's term as Treasury Secretary.

Respectfully, I would like to request that the FCIC investigate the claims made by former regulators William Black and Richard Newsom and determine whether Mr. Paulson's inaction constituted nonfeasance, which according to tort law is a passive failure to act when under an obligation to do so, or if his actions constituted misfeasance or even malfeasance, whereby Mr. Paulson actively took part in actions that caused harm and caused the financial meltdown. The Commission should kindly keep in mind that Mr. Paulson had the needed authority and influence to ensure our financial regulatory agencies put a stop to the risky lending practices that led to the crisis. Furthermore, I ask the Commission to determine whether the Office of Government Ethics explicitly allowed Mr. Paulson to keep millions in Goldman Sachs stock through his foundation while he was still serving as Secretary, or whether Mr. Paulson did so without government approval.

To the detriment of American taxpayers, Mr. Paulson has refused to comment on these serious charges. As such, I believe the FCIC is poised to shed light on the accusations surrounding Mr. Paulson's seemingly deliberate inaction and his clear conflicts of interest with former firm Goldman Sachs.

Thank you for your continued leadership as Chairman of the Financial Crisis Inquiry Commission and for the hard work the Commission has done on behalf of the American people. I look forward to the Commission's final report at the end of the year.

With kind regards, I am

Sincerely,

Cliff Stearns
United States Representative

CS:nda

Cc: the Honorable Bill Thomas, Commission Vice-Chairman

enclosure

–Four–
Quotes by Thomas Jefferson

The last quote by Jefferson (from 1802) is *remarkably* prescient.

> "When we get piled upon one another in large cities, as in Europe, we shall become as corrupt as Europe."

> "The democracy will cease to exist when you take away from those who are willing to work and give to those who would not."

> "It is incumbent on every generation to pay its own debts as it goes. A principle which if acted on would save one-half the wars of the world."

> "I predict future happiness for Americans if they can prevent the Government from wasting the labors of the people under the pretense of taking care of them."

> "My reading of history convinces me that most bad government results from too much government."

> "No free man shall ever be debarred the use of arms."

> "The strongest reason for the people to retain the right to keep and bear arms is, as a last resort, to protect themselves against tyranny in government."

> "The tree of liberty must be refreshed from time to time with the blood of patriots and tyrants."

> "To compel a man to subsidize with his taxes the propagation of ideas which he disbelieves and abhors is sinful and tyrannical."

> "I believe that banking institutions are more dangerous to our liberties than standing armies. If the American people ever allow private banks to control the issue of their currency, first by inflation, then by deflation, the banks and corporations

that will grow up around the banks will deprive the people of all property until their children wake-up homeless on the continent their fathers conquered..."

—

If you don't read the newspaper you are uninformed,
if you do read the newspaper you are misinformed.
—Mark Twain

–Five–
Tea Party quotes seen at protest marches

A patriot must always be ready to defend his country against his government.

Socialism is Trickle-Up Poverty

We the People are coming…We own the Dome

The desire to save humanity is always a front for the desire to rule it.

Ask not what your country can do for you….Ask what you can do yourself

Government off our Backs Now

DHS tip on spotting a right-wing extremist: watch out for the one carrying a paycheck

Spring cleaning tip: don't forget to change your scientific consensus from winter setting "climate change" to summer setting "global warming"

Kentucky Derby winner admits to having no specific strategy: I just kept repeating 'hope' and 'change' and I won… wow!

Congress nationalizes DeBeers, changes marketing slogan to 'government programs are forever'

Following Scotland's lead, US Justice Dept releases Charles Manson, citing battle with chronic hemorrhoids

Energy Czar: to save energy, the light at the end of the tunnel will be turned off

Don't spread the wealth… spread my work ethic

Obama appoints guilt czar to oversee fair distribution of guilt among all Am

Obama… Cuba Americans can recognize a socialize agenda

Study: Jesus spoke without a teleprompter

Congress… it is not your money.

Capitalism creates prosperity

New study suggests that 1 US gallon of Latte is 170 times more expensive than 1 US gallon of Regular gasoline

When the People fear the govt that's tyranny, when the govt fears the people that's freedom

Do not destroy the US with communist ideas

"I swear, by my life and my love of it, that I will never live for the sake of another man, nor ask another man to live for mine." –John Galt, Atlas Shrugged

Man is not free unless Govt is limited.

End the Fed

Stop spending my tax dollars like your earned them

Oust the Marxist usurper!.. His czars and thugs! Honduras did it!

–Six–

Why was no one prosecuted for contributing to the financial crisis?

by Bethany McLean
(Yahoo! Finance) finance.yahoo.com
March 12, 2016 8:35 AM

"This gags me." So said Elizabeth Warren in response to a Quora user, who asked, "What do you think are the real reasons that no Wall Street executives have been prosecuted for fraud as a result of the 2008 financial crisis?" Her answer, which she expounds on more thoroughly in her report Rigged Justice, is, "Weak enforcement begins at the top."

I've always thought the lack of prosecution was way more complicated than a simple lack of will, in part because there is a difference between criminally prosecutable behavior and that which is morally reprehensible. But I'm not sure whether we'll ever know the real answer. Newly public documents from the Financial Crisis Inquiry Commission show that the FCIC referred a handful of matters to the Justice Department for possible prosecution. Most of the time, nothing happened. In the cases where something did happen, our modern system of justice—the special one that applies to big business, that is—means that those of us on the outside—citizens, on whose behalf justice is supposed to be served—will never know the underlying truth.

Don't we at least deserve to understand?

Continue reading...

http://finance.yahoo.com/news/bethany-mclean-why-no-one-prosecuted-for-financial-crisis-fcic-new-documents-233806072.html

NEWS FROM
North Central Florida's Congressman
CLIFF STEARNS
For Immediate Release: December 22, 2008

STEARNS CALLS ON TREASURY SECRETARY TO END BAILOUT FOR FINANCIAL FIRMS THAT AWARDED TOP EXECUTIVES $1.6 BILLION IN COMPENSATION

ALSO CALLS ON PAUSLON TO AVOID EMPLOYMENT OR INVOLVEMENT WITH FIRMS PARTICIPATING IN BAILOUT

WASHINGTON, DEC. 22, 2008 – "It is outrageous that financial institutions benefiting from the taxpayer bailout awarded their top executives $1.6 billion in compensation last year," said Rep. Cliff Stearns (R-FL). "I call upon the Treasury Secretary to end taxpayer assistance to those firms that rewarded their executives for bringing them to insolvency. If that is not done, then Congress should take up the issue."

An Associated Press (AP) analysis found that firms receiving the taxpayer bailout provided nearly $1.6 billion in compensation to their top executives. The analysis found that this compensation included bonuses, stock options, use of company jets, home security systems, and memberships in country clubs.

"I can understand rewarding someone for doing a good job, but these executives guided these firms to near extinction and then turned to taxpayers for more funds," added Stearns. "According to the AP, the amount given to about 600 executives would cover the bailout costs for many of the 116 banks that accepted taxpayer dollars in the bailout."

Stearns also called on Treasury Secretary Paulson to reject any future job or involvement with any firm participating in the bailout. "I am concerned that the bailout of these financial institutions lacks transparency and a workable means of clearly avoiding a conflict of interest," concluded Stearns. "By taking this step, Paulson could set the tone that 'business as usual' on Wall Street has ended."

–Seven–

Big Banks Paid $110 Billion in Mortgage-Related Fines. Where Did the Money Go?

by Christina Rexrode and Emily Glazer
(Wall Street Journal) www.wsj.com
Updated March 9, 2016 4:07 p.m. ET

The nation's largest banks paid fines totaling about $110 billion for their role in inflating a mortgage bubble that helped cause the financial crisis. Where did that money go?

In New York, the annual state fair is using bank-settlement money to build a new horse barn and stables. In Delaware, proceeds are being used to subsidize email accounts for local police. In New Jersey, a mortgage firm owned by a former reality-television star collected $8.5 million as a reward for reporting a bank's misconduct.

Banks also helped tens of thousands of homeowners with their mortgages in neighborhoods from Jacksonville, Fla., to Riverside County, Calif., funded loans for low-income borrowers and donated to dozens of community groups and legal-aid organizations.

Yet some of the biggest chunks of money stayed with the entity that levied the fines in the first place. Of $109.96 billion of federal fines related to the housing crisis since 2010, roughly $50 billion ended up with the U.S. government with little disclosure of what happened next, according to a Wall Street Journal analysis.

The Journal reviewed the terms of more than 30 settlements, filed public-records requests with a dozen agencies at the federal and state level and spoke to dozens of homeowners and others who obtained payouts, tried to or were otherwise involved with the distribution of the settlements. The results represent the most detailed breakdown yet of the billions paid out in the unprecedented deals.

Continue reading…

http://www.wsj.com/articles/big-banks-paid-110-billionin-mortgage-related-fines-where-did-the-money-go-1457557442

NEWS FROM
North Central Florida's Congressman
CLIFF STEARNS
For Immediate Release: December 11, 2009

STEARNS VOTES NO ON HOUSE BILL MAKING CURRENT BAILOUT POLICIES PERMANENT

VOTES FOR ALTERNATIVE PLAN TO CURB ABUSES IN THE FINANCE INUDSTRY

WASHINGTON, DEC. 11, 2009 – "This legislation expands the powers of the very agencies that failed to catch the problems that created the financial crisis – it rewards a Federal Reserve that pursued irresponsible credit policies and that ineffectively conducted its regulatory supervision," stated Rep. Cliff Stearns (R-Sixth). "Shockingly, it also fails to reform either Fannie Mae and Freddie Mac, and it promotes inefficiency by blunting market discipline through government guarantees that protect creditors against loss. The bill also authorizes the taxation of businesses without the approval of Congress while making permanent the TARP (Troubled Asset Relief Program) policies that have squandered billions of taxpayer dollars."

"I supported the alternative plan that would end the bailout of financial institutions and that would create a new chapter in the bankruptcy code for non-bank financial institutions that would protect taxpayers from covering the greed and excesses of failing firms," explained Stearns.

The House today approved H.R. 4173, which permanently extends the bailout authorities used by the Treasury Department and the Federal Reserve to give taxpayer funds to the creditors and counterparties of failed Wall Street firms. In addition, the measure imposes a tax of $150 billion on large financial firms, many of which did not contribute to the financial crisis. The legislation also expands the power of the Federal Reserve Bank and creates a Credit Czar with authority to restrict access to credit and impose taxes on consumers and small businesses.

Added Stearns, "Instead of supporting this massive federal intrusion in the financial markets, I voted for an alternative that, in addition to creating a new chapter in the bankruptcy code, increases civil and criminal penalties for fraud, establishes a council to issue uniformed consumer protection rules, and reforms the over-the-counter derivatives market."

Stearns opposed establishing TARP and joined in urging Treasury Geithner to refrain from extending TARP into 2010, yet Geithner approved the extension of TARP. "The Inspector General For TARP has stated that the program lacks transparency, which prevents us from determining where the money is going and how it is spent," concluded Stearns. "Real reform means curbing questionable financial transactions and taking taxpayers off the hook for the failure of these firms."

*Attached is the official floor statement by Rep. Stearns on the causes of the financial crisis.

–Eight–

NEWS FROM
North Central Florida's Congressman
CLIFF STEARNS
For Immediate Release: November 4, 2011

STEARNS' INVESTIGATION RESULTS IN WHITE HOUSE SUBPOENA FOR SOLYNDRA DOCUMENTS

ADMINISTRATION'S CONTINUED STALLING FORCES THIS STEP TO ADVANCE INVESTIGATION

WASHINGTON, NOV. 4, 2011 – "Last night, the White House and the Office of Vice President were served with a subpoena for documents relating to the Solyndra loan guarantee," said Rep. Cliff Stearns (R-FL), Chairman of the House Energy and Commerce Committee's Subcommittee on Oversight and Investigations. "Unfortunately, we had to take this step after the White House has continued to slow walk the production of documents necessary for this investigation by only releasing selected documents and records."

The investigation into the loan guarantee has uncovered that numerous red flags were ignored in providing the funds to Solyndra, that taxpayers were subordinated to two private hedge firms in violation of the Energy Policy Act of 2005, and that political influence contaminated the loan guarantee process.

In explaining the subpoena, Stearns added, "This is an effort to get crucial documents to understand the role of the White House in the loan guarantee. We asked for all documents pertaining to communications with investors, on finalizing the loan guarantee, the financial condition of Solyndra, and the loan's restructuring. We have sent three letters to the White House seeking records, and this is the same information we requested in the October 5th letter. The subpoena provides until November 10th for the White House to share with us a schedule for producing the documents. I believe that the President owes it to the American people to explain in detail what happened to their tax money. In addition, as we work to promote job creation in our troubled economy, the failure of Solyndra offers important lessons to be learned."

–Nine–

BAILOUT MARKS KARL MARX'S COMEBACK
Posted: September 29, 2008, 8:03 PM by Jeff White
Martin Masse, mortgage crisis

Marx's Proposal Number Five seems to be the leading motivation for those backing the Wall Street bailout

By Martin Masse

In his Communist Manifesto, published in 1848, Karl Marx proposed 10 measures to be implemented after the proletariat takes power, with the aim of centralizing all instruments of production in the hands of the state. Proposal Number Five was to bring about the "centralization of credit in the banks of the state, by means of a national bank with state capital and an exclusive monopoly."

If he were to rise from the dead today, Marx might be delighted to discover that most economists and financial commentators, including many who claim to favour the free market, agree with him.

Continue reading at

http://www.wcvarones.com/2008/09/bailout-marx-article.html#more

–Ten–

When the American taxpayers look at the Troubled Asset Relief Program (TARP) and realize that the outlays could reach $1 trillion, they will naturally ask where did all the money go? Not only did the mission change within weeks of passage of this bill, but also the government began using the funds to buy equity positions in Wall Street banks rather than Main Street. It was a bait and switch tactic.

But here is the important point. An oversight panel found that $350 Billion of the TARP funds couldn't be accounted for! Here is the article describing this gross incompetence.

WHERE DID TAXPAYER MONEY GO? PANEL SLAMS TREASURY

By DANIEL ARNALL
ALICE GOMSTYN
ABC NEWS BUSINESS UNIT

Jan. 9, 2009

> A scathing new report by a congressional watchdog panel blames the Treasury Department for failing to track how banks are spending taxpayer money provided through the government's $700 billion financial rescue package, also known as the Troubled Asset Relief Program, or TARP.
>
> The panel, which has been charged with overseeing TARP and is led by Harvard Law professor Elizabeth Warren, said in its report that it "still does not know what the banks are doing with taxpayer money."
>
> By investing in banks that have refused "to provide any accounting of how they are using taxpayer money," the

Treasury Department has "eroded" public confidence, the report stated.

The panel also asked whether the Treasury Department, which has allocated more than $350 billion from the rescue package so far, failed to comply with Congress' instructions to tackle the country's foreclosure crisis.

The department took "no steps to use any of [the $700 billion rescue package] to alleviate the foreclosure crisis," and that "raises questions about whether Treasury has complied with Congress' intent that Treasury develop a 'plan that seeks to maximize assistance for homeowners,'" the report said.

Continue reading here:

http://abcnews.go.com/Business/Economy/story?id=6606296&page=1

Photographs

Press Conference in US Senate on Republican Healthcare plan alternate to Hillary-Care. Cliff was lead author of the legislation in the House of Representatives (at the podium) and Senator Don Nickles was the author in the Senate.

Muhammad Ali and Cliff after his testifying before Cliff's congressional subcommittee on boxing regulations reforms.

Republicans versus Democrat Basketball game at Gallaudet School for Deaf with Cliff MVP award for Republicans and Tom McMillen MVP award for Democrats-1989 (Democrats won!)

Magic Johnson plays basketball with members of Congress in their gym.

Ted Williams and Cliff at Ted's "Hitter's Hall of Fame Museum." Cliff represented the "The Splendid Splinter" in Congress. Ted lived in Inverness, Florida.

President Bush, Jeb Bush and Cliff at the Republican convention.

Dinner with Warren Buffett and afterwards he gives his wallet to Cliff in jest.

Sir Tim Berners-Lee invented the Internet. He met with Cliff after testifying at one of Cliff's congressional subcommittee hearings on the future of the Internet.

Index

527s (tax-exempt groups whose purpose is to influence elections), 46

A
Aeschylus, 100
Affordable Care Act (a.k.a. Obamacare), 73
   amendments to, 73–77
   Obama and budget neutrality of, 75–76
Afghanistan,
   liberation of, 21
   Russia at war in, 63
   U.S. started war in October, 2001, xiv
Air Force Congressional Caucus, 111
Alaska Light (Heacox), 41
Alchemist, The (Johnson), 56
Alexander the Great, 60
Alger Hiss case, 39
Allan, George, 38
Allen, James, 11
Alternative Energy and Advanced Transportation Financing Authority, California, 120
American International Group (AIG), 24, 87, 89, 104, 105, 106, 129, 142
American Recovery and Reinvestment Act of 2009, 120
American Revolution, 61, 85
national debt from financing, 115
American Sphinx: The Character of Thomas Jefferson (Ellis), 82

Ananias, 10
anarchy, 100
Andrews Air Force base, 110
Angelides, Phil, 130
Animal Farm (Orwell), 66
Antigone (Sophocles), 100
Arab Spring,
   originated in Tunisia, December, 2010, xiv
Argonaut Private Equity, 121
Aristotle, x, xi, xii, 15
Army, Dick, 31
As A Man Thinketh (Allen), 11
austerity, 82

B
Babeuf, François-Noël, 81
bad loans, 23, 24, 25, 126–129, 150–153
Bahrain,
   Arab Spring in, xiv
Baker, Richard, 57
Balkans,
   U.S. role in, 62
bank bailouts, 24, 25, 26, 27
   Keynesian economics as pretext for, 28
bank nationalization, 25
Bank of America Corp., 127, 128, 129, 150, 151, 153
Bank of America-Merrill Lynch deal, 126, 128
Barton, Joe, 32, 33, 34, 35, 36, 73, 74, 76

Base Realignment and Closure (BRAC) commission, 54
Bass, Charlie, 45
Bear Stearns Cos., 23, 24, 27, 123, 124, 127
Bellwether Consultants, 35
Bernanke, Ben S., 88, 127, 133, 136, 138
Bethesda Naval Hospital, 18
Bible, 10, 14
   acts of the Apostles, 10
   book of Genesis, 10
   book of Job, 10–11
   Epistle to the Galatians (Paul), 15
   Epistle to the Romans (Paul), 15
   letter to the Hebrews, 10
Big Short, The (movie), 107
bin Laden, Osama, 49
   killed in Pakistan in May, 2011, xiv
Bipartisan Policy Center, Washington, D.C., 149
Black, William, 130, 131, 133, 134, 135, 137
Black's Law Dictionary, 97
Blagojevich scandal, 59
Blankfein, Lloyd, 135
Blomquist, Michael, 135
Bloomberg Magazine, 123
Blunt, Roy, 26, 31, 32, 34, 35, 36
Bob Ney scandal, 45
Bobolink Foundation, 131, 135
Boehner, John, 31, 33, 35, 36, 46, 70, 119
Bolton, John, 60, 62
Bolton, Joshua, 87
Boston University School of Law, 103
Boys and Girls Club, 5
"Bridge to Nowhere", 40
British Empire, 60
budget committees (of Congress), 53
Burke, Edmund, xi
Burry, Michael, 107
Bush, George H. W.,
   1990 tax increases by, xiii

Bush, George H. W. IV, 87
Bush, George W., 38, 45, 48, 52, 53, 55, 57, 59, 63, 87, 89, 112, 133, 137
   elected president, November, 2000, xiii
   re-elected president, November, 2004, xiv
Bush, Jeb, 46
Business Week, 131

C

campaign finance bill, 8
cap and trade policy, 65
capitalism, 27
   controls and oversight in markets, 56
   thwarted by creeping socialism, 90
capital punishment, 80
Casa Grande's collective farm, Arizona (1930s), 66
categorical imperative, 9
Cellini, William, 59
challenging an incumbent, 31–32
Chambers, Whittaker, 39
Chapter 11 bankruptcy protection, 120, 121
Cheney, Dick, 53
Chocola, Chris, 45
Cicero, xi, 15
Citigroup Inc., 88, 135, 142, 143, 150, 151
citizen investigator role in Congress, 68
civic heritage, 61
civil rights, 16
Clayton Holdings, 143, 144, 146
Clinton, Bill, 78, 87, 88, 96, 97, 98, 99
   elected president, November, 1992, xiii
   impeachment of, December, 1998, xiii, 78–80
   re-elected president, November, 1996, xiii
CMEA Ventures, 121
code of ethics (for Congress), 86
collateralized debt obligations (CDOs), 106

Communism, 15
Comptroller General of the United
    States, 51, 52, 54
conflict of interest, 87–89, 106
Congress,
    bailouts, 27
    budget Committees of, 53
    career in, 2, 3, 4
    challenges, 1–2
    choices on leaving, 2–3
    citizen investigator primary role
        in, 68
    Committee chairs in, 7
    conflict-of-interest test needed in, 87
    debt reduction, 28
    deficit reduction, 28
    impeachment referral sent,
        September, 1988, 79
    importance of steering Committee
        in, 18
    incumbent challenges in, 31–32
    interest in higher office from
        members of, 2–3
    legislative insider primary role in, 68
    lobbying and, 86–87
    membership process, 1–2
    money rather than politics at center
        of, 86–88
    natural laws and, 11
    once elected to, 17–18
    outsider primary role in, 68, 69–70
    party insider primary role in, 68
    sacred responsibility of members
        of, x
    spiraling debt and, 119
    statesman primary role in, 68, 69
    sunset government programs, 114
    travel perks for members of, 108–110
    understanding own strengths and
        weakness as a member of, 70
    voting choices in, 9–10
    Ways and Means Committee, 2
congressional campaign,
    events following, 17–19
    fundraising for, 5–6, 58–59
    strategies, 6–7
Congressional Clerk Hire Funds, 39
conservatorship, 124
continuing resolution (CR), 53
copper indium gallium selenide
    (CIGS), 120
corruption, 12
Countrywide Savings and Loan, 137
coup d'état, 31
Cavicke, Dave, 34, 35
Creighton, Francis, 149
crimes of vengeance, 100
culture of risk, 65
Cunningham, Duke, 45, 48
Cuomo, Andrew, 151, 152

D

Davidoff, Steven M., 125, 126
DCI Group, 58
DealBook, 125
Deal Professor blog, The, 125
debt-driven fiscal policy, 84
Declaration of Independence, 15, 82
    freedom or liberty expressed in, 21
Delay, Tom, 31
democracy, 13
    freedom in, 14
    spreading of, 62
Democratic Party, ix
    "Big Bang" agenda of, 66
    takes control of House of
        Representatives, January, 2007,
        xiv, 65
Democratic Vistas (Whitman), 41
Department of Defense (DOD), 52
    budget of, 51, 54
Department of Energy, 120, 121
Department of Justice, 117, 142, 145,
    147, 148, 149, 150, 151, 152, 153
    Civil Division, 146
depression (financial), 29
    under Franklin D. Roosevelt, 89

de Tocqueville, Alexis, xi
Dingell, John, 68, 119
Disney World, 35
divine law, 100–101
divine retribution (punishment), 9, 10
   education and love follow, 10
   prevalent ethos and, 12–13
   suffering and, 10–11
Dodd, Chris, 26
Dodd-Frank legislation, 107
"Dominion of Providence over the Passions of Men, The", 61
Drake, Thelma, 46
Dugan, John, 137
Duke Cunningham scandal, 45
DuVally, Michael, 136

E
Egypt,
   Arab Spring in, xiv
Ellis, Joseph, 82, 83
Emergency Economic Stabilization Act of 2008, 102
Energy and Commerce Committee, The, 32, 33–34, 36
   Commerce, Trade and Consumer Protection Subcommittee, 117
   Oversight and Investigations Subcommittee, 116–117, 119
   Telecommunications and Internet Subcommittee, 32, 36
England,
   evolution of constitutional authority in, 83
Enron, 37, 56, 117
Erasmus, Desiderius, 119, 121
étatism (statecontrol/socialism), 65
ethical behavior, 12, 45, 130–132
   campaign contributions area of risk, 47
   congressional ethics manual, 48
   congressional work balance with campaign or political work area of risk, 47
   constituent services area of risk, 47–48
   daily risks, 47–48
   gifts and travel area of risk, 47
   sexual impropriety risk area, 48
Eton Park Capital Management LP, 123
eudaimonia (happiness), x
exceptionalism, 60, 61, 62, 64
expansionism, 62
Extraordinary Popular Delusions & the Madness of Crowds (Mackay), 56

F
fall of Berlin Wall (November, 1989), xiii
Federal Budget, 51–54
   flaws in, 52, 54
Federal Bureau of Investigation (FBI), 120, 134
Federal Deposit Insurance Corporation (FDIC), 24, 25, 90, 103
Federal Election Commission, 58
Federal Home Loan Bank, San Francisco, 137
Federal Home Loan Mortgage Corporation *(Freddie Mac)*, 24, 26, 27, 55, 57, 58, 90, 115, 116, 117, 118, 123, 124, 135, 137, 148, 150, 151
Federal Housing Finance Agency (FHFA), 26, 150
Federal Housing Finance Reform Act of 2005, 26
federalism, 82–83
   Jefferson's ideas on, 82–84
   as limit to federal government, 113
Federalist Papers, xi, 86, 102
Federalist Society, 103
Federal National Mortgage Association *(Fannie Mae)* (FNMA), 24, 26, 27, 55, 57, 58, 90, 115, 116, 117, 118, 123, 135, 137, 143, 148, 150, 151
Federal Reserve, 27, 90, 106, 124, 127
Feldstein, Stephen, 88

finances of federal government, 51–54
finance.yahoo.com, 142
Financial Accounting Standards Board (FASB), 55, 56, 117
Financial Crisis Inquiry Commission (FCIC), 106, 130, 131, 132, 136, 138, 142, 143, 144, 145
Financial Industry Reform Act, 90
Financial Market Commission, 104
"Financial Report of the United States Government", 51
  December 17, 2007, 51–52
  September, 2008, 52, 53
Financial Services Roundtable, 149
Fitzgerald, Peter, 59
Foley, Mark, 31, 45
Foster, Vincent, 80
Frank, Barney, 26, 57
Frankfurter, Felix, 95
freedom, 14
  of choice and self-determination, 14
  compared to liberty, 21
  for excellence, 14
  as expressed in Declaration of Independence, 21
  spreading of, 62
  thoughts on, 41–42
  types of, 14–16
Freedom of Information Act requests, 136
free market economy, 23, 25, 65
French Revolution, 80
Friedman, Jen, 149
Friedman, Milton, 66, 88
Friedman, Stephen, 105
fundraising, 5–6
  after successful congressional campaign, 19
  campaign finance bill and, 8
  congressional campaign, 5–6
  effects of, 7–8
  fundraisers and, 7
  name recognition and, 40

scandals, 7–8

G

Gadsden flag, 14
Gainesville Sun, 95
Gallatin, Albert, 84
Geithner, Timothy, 87, 88
George Kaiser Family Foundation, 121
Gephardt, Dick, 99
Gingrich, Newt, 7, 27, 31, 33, 70, 78, 79, 80, 81
Glass-Steagall Act, 89, 90, 106
Glazer, Emily, 147
globalism, 28
global warming legislation, 35
gnothi seauton (know thyself), 70
Goldman Sachs Group Inc., 23, 27, 87, 88, 90, 105, 106, 124, 129, 130, 131, 133, 134, 135, 136, 142, 150
Gordon, Greg, 133
Government Accountability Office (GAO), 153
government of limited powers, 102–104
government-sponsored enterprises (GSEs), 57, 115–116, 125
Great Depression, 133
Green, Eric, 153
Greenspan, Alan, 90, 116, 136, 138
Greg, Judd, 26
gross domestic product (GDP), x
Gulf War (August 1990–February 1991), xiii

H

Hagel, Chuck, 58
Hamilton, Alexander, 84, 115
Harris, Kamala, 152
Harris, Katharine, 46
Hart, Melissa, 46
Hastert, Dennis, 31, 32, 45, 48, 49, 55, 56, 57, 59
Hayworth, J. D., 46
Heacox, Kim, 41
Healthcare and Energy legislation, 36

Herodotus, 12, 13
heroism, 65
Histories of Herodotus, 12, 13
History of England, The (Hume), 83
Homeland Security Committee, 7
homosexuality, 45
House Committee on Appropriations, 6, 7, 53, 54, 85, 109
House of Representatives,
　compromises in, 9
　Democratic Party takes control of, January, 2007, xiv
　Education and Labor Committee, 74
　Energy Commerce Committee, 55, 74
　Financial Institutions Committee (prev. Banking Committee), 55, 56
　Financial Services Committee, 117
　first-time voting in, 19–20
　importance of, ix
　International Affairs Committee, 109
　Judiciary Committee, 79
　means of Republican Party keeping control of, 82–84
　as most accountable of federal government, ix
　party affiliation in, ix
　powers of, ix, x
　Republican Party loses control of in November, 2006, 45
　Republican Party takes control of in January, 1995, xiii
　Republican Party takes control of in January, 2011, xiv, 82
　Speaker of, 55
　Supreme Court and, ix
　temptation, immorality and ethical challenges in, 20
　Transportation Committee, 109, 110
　voting record in, 34
　Ways and Means Committee, 74
　work of, ix
House Oversight and Government Reform Committee, 126
housing real estate market, 56
Hume, David, 83
Hussein, Saddam, 50
Hyde, Henry, 79, 80

I

impeachment of president, ix, 96, 97–98, 99
imperial presidency, 113
Independent Counsel Act, 96
Independent Party, 18, ix
individual retirement account (IRA), 23
IndyMac Bank, 137
innovation, 65
In Praise of Folly (Erasmus), 119, 121
insolvency of savings banks, 23–25
Inspector General (IG), Treasury Department, 29
Institutional Risk Analytics, 137
International Monetary Fund, 137
Iran, 39
　nuclear program in, 63
Iraq,
　defining what post-war success meant in, 48
　Desert Storm in, 62
　emergency appropriations for the war in, 48
　invasion of without exit strategy, 50
　liberation of, 21
　no intellectual case made for war in, 49
　President Obama orders end of military involvement in, October, 2011, xiv
　second war started in, March, 2003, xiv
　U.S. invasion of, 45
　war as clash of civilizations, 49
　war in, 112
Isaac, William M., 25, 26
Islam, 92

Islamists, 49
Israel,
    U.S. influence in, 63

J
Jefferson, Thomas, 15, 82, 83, 84, 85,
    112, 113, 115, 118
    quotations, 139–140
Jimmy Miller Worldwide Travel
    Club, 110
Johnson, Ben, 56
Johnson, Keith, 144
Johnson, Lyndon B., 50
Johnson, Nancy, 46
Johnson, Norma, 98
Jordan,
    Arab Spring in, xiv
J.P. Morgan Chase & Co., 123, 127, 128,
    150, 151
Julius Caesar, 60

K
Kant, Immanuel, 9
Kavanaugh, Brett, 80
Keynes, John Maynard, 27, 28, 29,
    30, 104
Keynesian economic theory, 28, 104
    alternatives to, 29–30
    definition of, 29
Khomeini, Ayatollah, 49
King, Peter, 7
King David, 10
Klein, Aaron, 149
Kolbe, Jim, 45
Koran, xi
Korea,
    U.S. role in, 62
K Street (lobbyists), 32, 34, 35, 57

L
LaHood, Ray, 59
Lawson, Gary S., 103
legal process, 95
legislative insider role in Congress, 68

Lehman Brothers, 23, 127, 129
Lewinsky, Monica, 80
Lewis, Ken, 127, 128
liberty,
    civil, 61
    compared to freedom, 21
    nation emerged from concept of, 60
Libya,
    Arab Spring in, xiv
Lincoln, Abraham, 85
Lincoln Savings and Loan debacle,
    130, 134
Livingston, Bob, 85
Lojek, Karen, 154
Lone Pine Capital LLC, 124
Lord Acton, 84
Lott, Trent, 78, 79, 80
Louis XIV, King of France, 60
Ludgren, Dan, 2

M
Mackay, Charles, 56
Madison, James, 102, 113
Madrone Capital Partners, 121
Main Street, 89, 130
majority rule, 14
    truth and, 16
Mandel, Stephen, 124
Manson, Charles, 141
march of freedom, xi
Mark Foley scandal, 31, 45
Marshall Plan, 62
Martinez, Mel, 35
Masdar and Artis Capital
    Management, 121
material adverse change (MAC) clause,
    127, 128
Maurer, Diana, 153
McCain, John, 69
McClatchy Newspapers, 133, 134
McClintock, Tom, 2
McDonnell, Bob, 48
McLean, Bethany, 142
Medicaid, 82, 112

Medicare, 74, 82, 112
member of Congress (MC), 2
Merrill Lynch, 126, 128, 129, 142
Miami Herald, The, 130, 133
Middle East, 63
Miller, Jimmy, 110
Mindich, Eric, 124
minimalist theory of government (Thomas Jefferson), 83
Mizer, Benjamin, 146
monarchy, 13
morality, 16, 48, 113
Morgan Stanley, 23, 145, 146, 147
Mortgage Finance, 137
Mount Vernon, 61
MoveOn.org, 46
Muhammad, 49
Muir, John, 42

N

Natcher, Bill, 6
national debt, 84
National Republican Congressional Committee (NRCC), 32, 33, 35
Native Americans, 62, 101
natural laws, 10
  obedience and, 11
Naval Bethesda Hospital, 6
Nazism, 15
Negroponte, John, 50
Newsom, Richard, 130, 131, 134
Newsweek, 88
New Testament, 9, 10
New York Times, 124
Ney, Bob, 45, 48
Nixon, Richard, 39, 50
No Child Left Behind Act of 2001 (NCLB), 48
non-commission officer (NCO), 110
North American Free Trade Agreement (NAFTA),
  signed into law, January, 1994, xiii
Northrop, Ann, 46

O

Obama, Barak, 36, 52, 54, 57–58, 59, 60, 62, 63, 66, 87, 88, 89, 120, 121
  elected president, November, 2008, xiv, 65
  orders end of U.S. military involvement in Iraq, October, 2011, xiv
  re-elected president, November, 2012, xiv
obstruction of justice, 96
Och, Daniel, 124
Och-Ziff Capital Management Group LLC, 124
Office of Management and Budget (OMB), 49
Office of the Comptroller of the Currency, 124, 136, 137
Office of Thrift Supervision, 136, 137
Old Testament, 9–10
oligarchy, 13
On the Shortness of Life (Seneca), 12
Oresteia (Aeschylus), 100
Orlando Sentinel, 37
Ottoman Empire, 49
outsider role in Congress, 68, 69–70
Owen, Robert, 92
Oxley, Michael, 56, 57

P

Paine, Tom, 64
parochialism, 11
party affiliation,
  in House of Representatives, ix
  in Senate, ix
party insider role in Congress, 68
Patient Protection and Affordable Care Act ("Obamacare"),
  signed into law, March, 2010, xiv
patriotism, 60
Paul, 15
Paulson, Henry (Hank) M., Jr., 23, 24, 26, 27, 52, 87, 88, 89, 123, 124, 125, 126, 130, 131, 133, 134, 136, 137, 138

Paulson, Henry, 135
Paulson, Wendy, 135
Paulson ethic conflict, 130–132
"Paulson Predicament", 26
Paxton, Bill, 31
Pelosi, Nancy, 24, 26
Pence, Mike, 25
perjury, 96
   penalties for, 97
Peters, Morris, 152
Petraeus, David, 50
Pickering, Chip, 78
Pitts, Joe, 75
planned government investment, 30
Plato, 15
plutocracy, 113
polis (Greek city state), x
political action committees (PACs), 7, 34, 59
Politics (Aristotle), 15
Pontius Pilate, 16
pork barreling, 57
power corrupts; absolute power corrupts absolutely, 84
predictive business cycle, 29–30
president of the United States (POTUS), 6
   impeachment of, ix
Princeton University, 61
Protestant Reformation, 14
publicity, 37–40
   daily press releases, 39
   fundraising and, 40
   national television and radio, 38–39
   newsletters, 39–40
   sound bites, 37–38
   telethons, 39
   websites, 39
   writing op-ed for local newspaper, 37

Q
Quayle, Dan, 39

R
Raines, Franklin, 56
Rand, Ayn, 56
rationalism (18th century), 14
Reagan, Ronald, 60, 61, 63, 85
rebellion, 61
recession, 29
   2007 recession, xiv, 87
   2008 recession, 51
Redpoint Ventures, xiv, 121
Reid, Harry, 26
reinvention, 65
republican form of government, 82
Republican Party, ix
   freemarket economy and, 25
   "Free to Choose" paradigm of, 66
   loses control of House of Representatives, November, 2006, 45
   means of keeping control of House of Representatives, 82–84
   members of as free marketeers, 23
   retiring national debt as highest priority, 84
   takes control of House of Representatives, January, 1995, xiii
   takes control of House of Representatives, January, 2011, 65, 82
   trying to amend Obamacare bill, 73–75
Republic (Plato), 15
Reserve Primary Fund money market, 23, 24
residential mortgage-backed security (RMBS), 145, 146
Resolution Trust Corporation, 104
Reuters, 144
Rexrode, Christina, 147
Rezko, Tony, 59
rhetoric, 69
Rice, Condoleezza, 38

right thinking, 11, 12
Robespierre, Maximilien, 80
RockPort Capital Partners, 121
Rodenbush, Patrick, 151
Rogers, Mike, 75, 76
Roman Empire, 83
Roosevelt, Franklin D., 89
Rove, Karl, 46
Rubin, Robert, 87, 88
Ruff, Charles, 97
rule of law, 95, 100, 101, 113
   perjury as direct assault on, 96
rule of reason, x
Rumsfield, Donald, 46, 48
Runyan, Bob, 150
Russia, 39

S
Saladin, 49
Sapphira, 10
Sarbanes-Oxley Act of 2002, 137
Saudi Arabia, 38, 39
   Arab Spring in, xiv
Saul, 10
Savings and Loans (S&L) crisis, 24, 56, 104, 135, 137
scandals,
   Blagojevich, 59
   Bob Ney, 45, 48
   Duke Cunningham, 45, 48
   Jim Kolbe, 45
   Mark Foley, 31, 45
schmoozing, 69
Schumpeter, Joseph, 89, 90
Senate,
   Banking Committee, 116
   party affiliation in, ix
Seneca, 12
separation of church and state, 12
September, 2001 (9/11) terrorist attacks, xiv
Setting Course: A Congressional Management Guide, 48
Sharia law, 49

Shaw, Clay, 46
Shays, Chris, 69
Shearman & Sterling, 125
Shelby, Richard, 26
Sherwood, Don, 46
Shimkus, John, 32
Silicon Valley, 135
Simmons, Ron, 46
simplicity, 82
Singh, Dinakar, 124
slavery, 62, 101
Slumdog Millionaire (movie), 58
socialism, 81
   creeping, 90
   spread of, 93
   Western European, 94
   world, 92–93
socialization of healthcare, 65, 66
Solyndra, 120, 121
Solyndra investigation, 119–121
Sophocles, 100
sound bites, 37–38
South Africa,
   end of *apartheid* in, April 1994, xiii
Special Purpose Entities, 56
Stamford law school, 34
Stanford, Mark, 3
Stark, Rodney, 49
Starr, Kenneth, 79, 80, 96, 97, 98
2007 Statement on Social Security, 52
State of the Union Address, 78
statesman role in Congress, 68, 69
statism, 66
Stearns, Cliff, 95, 98
steering committee,
   decisions of could affect careers, 19
   importance of, 18
   makeup of, 18
Stevens, Ted, 40
Supreme Court,
   House of Representatives and, ix
Swecker, Chris, 134
Sykes-Picot agreement (1916), 49

Syria,
    Arab Spring in, xiv

T

T. Rowe Price, 23
ta genomena ex anthropon (things that result from human action), 13
Tauzin, Billy, 56, 57
Taylor, Charles, 46
Taylor, John, 112
Tea Party, 90
    quotations, 140–141
Teitelbaum, Richard, 123
theocracy, 49
Third World socialist regimes, 93
Thomas, Bill, 132
Three Percent Fund, 153
Tiananmen Square protests, Beijing (April–June, 1989), xiii
Time magazine, 55
totalitarianism, 15
Tower of Babel, 10
TPG-Axon Capital Management LP, 124
Treasury Department, 24, 123, 124, 125, 148, 150
Troubled Asset Relief Program (TARP) bailout, 23, 27, 28, 89, 128
truth, 16
    importance for justice, 96
Tunisia,
    Arab Spring originates in, December 2010, xiv
Twain, Mark, 140
tyranny, 95, 100

U

UBS, 143
unalienable rights, 15
Union of Soviet Socialist Republics (Soviet Union),
    collapse of, December, 1991, xiii, 93
United Nations (UN), 50, 64
United Way, 5

universal laws, 9
University of Connecticut School of Law, 125
University of Missouri-Kansas City, 137
Upton, Fred, 32
U.S. Constitution of 1788, 21, 62, 83, 103
    impeachment in, 97
U.S. Securities and Exchange Commission (SEC), 55, 117, 128, 131, 134, 135, 137, 143
US Venture Partners, 121

V

Victory of Reason, The: How Christianity Led to Freedom, Capitalism and Western Success (Stark), 49
Virgin Green Fund, 121
voting (in Congress),
    considerations, 9
    repercussions of, 9–10
    truth and, 16

W

Waffner, Troy, 152
Walker, David, 51, 52, 54
Wall Street, 27, 28, 56, 87, 88, 105, 106, 124, 130, 133, 135, 137, 142, 143
Wall Street Journal, 88, 145, 147, 148, 150, 152
WaMu, 137
Warren, Elizabeth, 142
Washington, George, 60, 61, 64
Washington Mutual, 24
Waxman, Henry, 73, 74, 75
Weld, William, 97
Weldon, Curt, 46
Wells Fargo & Co., 150
Western civilization,
    value of, x
Whalen, Christopher, 137
whistleblowers, 39
Whitewater, 80
Whitfield, Ed, 32

Whitman, Walt, 41
Will, George, 24, 90
Winthrop, John, 61, 64
Wisdom of Crowds, 39
Witherspoon, John, 16, 61
witness tampering, 96
World Bank, 88
World War II (WWII), 62
World War I (WWI), 62

Y

Yemen,
   Arab Spring in, xiv
Young, Bill, 47, 85

About the Author

Cliff Stearns is an Executive Director based in APCO Worldwide's Washington, DC, office and serves as a member of APCO's International Advisory Council. *Recently he was elected President of the United States Association of Former Members of Congress (USAFMC).* He is a former Member of Congress for Florida's 6th district, where he gained extensive experience in telecommunications, technology, cybersecurity and international trade during his twenty-four years of service.

Congressman Stearns was also a business owner of motels and restaurants before being elected to Congress. As chair of the Energy & Commerce Oversight and Investigations Subcommittee, he helped increase transparency in the federal government and led the Solyndra investigation. Congressman Stearns served as the Republican leader on the Communications, Technology and Internet Subcommittee and was Chairman of the Subcommittee on Commerce, Manufacturing and Trade, where he enacted consumer privacy and data security legislation.

He is a graduate of the George Washington University with a degree in electrical engineering. He was a captain in the United States Air Force and served four years as an aerospace project engineer providing satellite reconnaissance of Vietnam. He was awarded the Air Force Commendation Medal for distinguished service and meritorious achievement and later, as a Congressman, received the Air Force Association W. Stuart Symington Award, the highest honor presented to a civilian in the field of national security.

Mr. Stearns lives in Ocala, Florida, with his wife Joan. He and Joan have three grown sons.

Endnotes

1. Anthony Kenny, *Aristotle on the Perfect Life* (Oxford, 1992).

2. Robert Barron, *Word on Fire: Proclaiming the Power of Christ* (New York: Crossroad Publishing Company, 2008).

3. https://en.wikipedia.org/wiki/As_a_Man_Thinketh

4. E. Marie Bothé, *Be Right of Go Wrong: A Fundamentally Different Way of Life Taught by Richard W Wetherill* (Royersford PA: Alpha Publishing House, 1996).

5. Ibid., 31.

6. Seneca, *On the Shortness of Life* (New York: Penguin Great Ideas, 2005), 84.

7. Ibid., 93.

8. Daniel Mendelsohn, "Arms and the Man." (Review-essay on *Herodotus* and *The Landmark Herodotus*.) *New Yorker*, 28 April, 2008.

9. Barron, *Word on Fire*

10. Everett Wilson, "Alienable Rights" *Partial Observer*, www.partialobserver.com/article.cfm?id=312.

11. James Surowiecki, *The Wisdom of Crowds* (Anchor, 2005).

12. Barron, *Word on Fire*, 213.

13. Robin Sharma, *The Monk Who Sold His Ferrari* (San Francisco: Harper Collins, 1999)

14. George Will, "Our Federal Economy" *Washington Post*, September 27, 2008.

15. William M Isaac, "A Better Way To Aid Banks," *Washington Post*, September 27, 2008. [Isaac was former Chairman of FDIC from 1981 to 1985.]

16. Cliff Stearns, "Stearns: Our efforts to protect Florida's coastline," *Orlando Sentinel*, October 2, 2005.

17 Surowiecki, *Wisdom of Crowds*, 119.

18 Kim Heacox, *Alaska Light*, (Portland OR: Graphic Arts Books, 1998)

19 https://en.wikipedia.org/wiki/Democratic_Vistas

20 Heacox, *Alaska Light*, 13

21 Ibid., 27.

22 Ibid., 35.

23 Ibid., 48.

24 Ibid., 68.

25 Ibid., 75.

26 David Twenhafel, ed., *Setting Course: A Congressional Management Guide*. 4th ed. (Washington, D.C.: Congressional Management Foundation, 1992)

27 Ibid., 272.

28 Don Wolfensberger, "A House Divided" (review of *The Broken Branch* by Mann and Ornstein) *Wilson Quarterly*, Autumn 2006.

29 George Will, "A lesson in irrational exuberance" Washington Post, November 11, 2006. [Sec. of Defense's Dick Cheney's comments: "Once you've got Baghdad, it's not clear what you do with it."]

30 Efraim Karsh, *Islamic Imperialism*, (New Haven: Yale University Press, 2006), 207–208.

31 Ibid., 209

32 Rodney Stark, *The Victory of Reason: How Christianity Led to Freedom, Capitalism, and Western Success* (New York: Random House, 2007)

33 David Walker, Budget Director, "Financial Report of the United Sates Government 2007"

34 Ibid.

35 https://en.wikipedia.org/wiki/Extraordinary_Popular_Delusions_and_the_Madness_of_Crowds

36 https://en.wikipedia.org/wiki/The_Alchemist_(play)

37 Pete Yost, "Freddie Mac Investigates self over lobby campaign," Associated Press, February 23, 2009.

38 John H. Fund, "LaHood's Neighborhood," *American Spectator,* March 2009

39 Interview with Edward Luce of the *Financial Times,* April 4, 2009

40 Joshua Muravchik, *Heaven on Earth: The Rise and Fall of Socialism* (San Francisco: Encounter Books, 2003)

41 Ibid.

42 Ibid.

43 Barack Obama, Inaugural Address, January 21, 2009.

44 Twenhafel, *Setting Course,* 128.

45 Ibid., 136

46 Joseph J. Ellis *American Sphinx: The Character of Thomas Jefferson* (New York: Knopf, 2005), 215.

47 Ibid., 183.

48 Ibid., 194.

49 Ibid.

50 Ibid., 196.

51 Ibid., 186.

52 Robin Rubin, "Getting the Economy Back on Track," www.newsweek.com, December 29, 2009.

53 Arianna Huffington, *Third World America: How Our Politicians Are Abandoning the Middle Class and Betraying the American Dream* (New York: Broadway Books, 2011), 150.

54 Muravchik, *Heaven on Earth*

55 Ibid.

56 Ibid., 333.

57 Ibid., 324.

58 Ibid.

59   United States Supreme Court UNITED STATES v. UNITED MINE WORKERS OF AMERICA, (1947) No. 759

60   Anthony O'Hear, *Great Books: A Journey Through 2500 years of the West's Classic Literature* (Wilmington DE: Intercollegiate Studies Institute, 2009), 45.

61   Ibid., 57.

62   The Federalist No. 45 (James Madison), at 292 (Clinton Rossiter ed., 1961). Quoted from Lawson (see below)

63   Gary S. Lawson, "Limited Government, Unlimited Administration: Is it Possible to Restore Constitutionalism?" *Heritage Foundation* No. 23 January 27, 2009

64   Dave Breese, *Seven Men Who Rule the World from the Grave* (Chicago: Moody Press, 1990).

65   Shah Gilani, "Warning: This is not another Wall Street Conspiracy Theory, These are the Facts" Money Morning, February 2, 2010 – moneymorning.com

66   Ibid.

67   Ibid.

68   Ibid.

69   Ibid.

70   Ibid.

71   Ibid.

72   Ibid.

73   http://nymag.com/daily/intelligencer/2015/12/big-short-genius-says-another-crisis-is-coming.html

74   Thomas Jefferson to John Taylor, 1798. ME 10:64 [N.B. *The Writings of Thomas Jefferson*, (Memorial Edition) Lipscomb and Bergh, editors]

75   Thomas Jefferson to James Madison, 1789. ME 7:455

76   Ibid., ME 7:454

77   Ibid., ME 7:455

78   Ibid., ME 7:457

79 William J. Quirk, "Just One More Thing" *Chronicles,* May 09.

80 John Willson "Adams' Federalism"; Clyde Wilson, "A Limited Presidency"; and Stephen B. Presser, "Reviewing Judicial Review," *Chronicles* May 09

81 Isaiah 11:1-3 "The seven gifts of the Holy Spirit"

82 Barron, *Word on Fire*

83 Thomas Jefferson to John Taylor, 1816. ME 15:23 84 en.wikipedia.org/wiki/Solyndra

85 Ibid.

86 "According to a preliminary legal analysis prepared for the Department of Energy (DOE) by outside counsel, subordination of the loan guarantee was prohibited under the 2005 Energy Policy Act. DOE chose not to have the legal analysis finalized, instead developing an internal justification that was finalized only after the restructuring had been agreed to." (source November 17, 2011 Energy & Commerce Press Release)

87 en.wikipedia.org/wiki/Solyndra

88 Ibid.

89 Ibid.

90 Ibid.